DATE DUE

Also by Patrick J. Smith

∽

THE TENTH MUSE

*A Historical Study of the
Opera Libretto*

A Year at the Met

A Year at the Met

Patrick J. Smith

ALFRED A. KNOPF

New York 🐕 *1983*

THIS IS A BORZOI BOOK

PUBLISHED BY ALFRED A. KNOPF, INC.

Library of Congress Cataloging in Publication Data
Smith, Patrick J., 1932–
A year at the Met.
Includes index.
1. Metropolitan Opera (New York, N.Y.) I. Title.
ML1711.8.N3M62   1983   782.1'09747'1   82-47829
ISBN 0-394-51783-0

Manufactured in the United States of America
First Edition

Contents

Contents

Contents

Preface

I decided to write this book because I wanted to study the way a repertory house functions: a repertory house that performs opera, in New York, in 1981–82. I wanted a season under the artistic control of the present management, and reflective of their aims, and I wanted a season that was more or less normal. I had originally planned to write the book about 1980–81, but the lockout and curtailment of performances resulted in a highly abnormal season. Although 1981–82 was still somewhat affected by the residue of the lockout, it was largely what had been planned by the management.

This book is not an authorized one, in the sense of carrying a Metropolitan Opera imprimatur. I wished to retain the freedom to discuss all aspects of the opera season, and therefore chose to write this book from an "outside" point of view, albeit one in general sympathy. Yet I received cooperation from everyone in the opera house, and particularly from those in the press office, whom I doubtless wearied with my eternal questions. I spoke to many more people than those whose names are given in the book, from outside the Met, backstage, and on the Met's board. My thanks to them, and to my old friend (and executive committee member and secretary of the board) Alton E. Peters, who corrected more than one inaccuracy. I must add that during my research I met with an open frankness that I had not expected to find.

My thanks also to David Hamilton, who read the manuscript and offered many valuable suggestions.

Finally, I must here confess my indebtedness to one book which

I have long considered a major study of the theater: William Gold-man's analysis of a single Broadway season entitled *The Season* (New York, 1969). Goldman took each production and used it as a springboard to discuss an aspect of Broadway, and I have shame-lessly (but gratefully) appropriated his format for my book.

My book is hardly all-inclusive, though it touches on most if not all of the many themes that are intertwined in an operatic reper-tory season. If it leads to a fuller understanding of repertory opera in the 1980s, and opera at the Met, and places that company in today's operatic and cultural world, I shall feel amply rewarded.

A Year at the Met

Introduction

The Metropolitan Opera presents opera in repertory—in the 1981–82 season, for thirty weeks of seven performances a week. It is a museum of past operatic history: a museum that presents some—but not all—of the masterpieces of the past, and some minor examples as well. It presents very few contemporary works. It presents operas that have a track record of popularity, operas that appeal to singers, and operas that the management feels are part of what the Metropolitan Opera should be performing, whether popular or not.

Yet, despite the sheer number of its performances over those seasons, and despite the lists of works and of the singers who have appeared in them (including a majority of the great opera singers of those years), Virgil Thomson could nonetheless write that during his tenure at the *Herald Tribune* the Met was "not a part of New York's intellectual life" (New York *Herald Tribune*, November 16, 1952).* He was correct then, and the statement is probably still true. The newest intellectual ideas, in opera or in opera production, will not be seen at the Met. It has continued as a repository of the past rather than as a trendsetter, and prefers, as a museum, to carry the weight of its own history.

If the Met, then, is confined in its artistic role within the community, what justifies its existence? Why should space be devoted to its doings—why, in short, should Virgil Thomson be interested in commenting on it?

---

*Reprinted in *Music Reviewed* (New York, 1967), p. 355.

Because, as the mountain climber said, it is there. It is there to the bulk of a $66 million annual budget (the Metropolitan Opera Guild, its primary support organization, has a $9 million-a-year budget), playing to almost three-quarters of a million people annually in the Lincoln Center house, to additional thousands on tour and in the summer parks concerts, and to millions via radio and television. It is there because it presents a representative cross section of operas, with casts that include many of the top singers of the day; and it is there because its constant performing activity generates publicity that carries throughout the United States and Canada and throughout Western Europe: a successful debut at the Met, or a Met triumph, can still change a singer's or a conductor's life, and will certainly change his or her fee scale. It is there because, as a museum, it performs a museum function of presenting operas in repertory to an extent unmatched in the United States.

The word "repertory" is integral to the Met, and it should be more closely defined.

"Repertory" is a slippery word, used in differing senses when discussing opera. It is often used by companies that are not in the dictionary sense repertory companies. The strict definition of the American College Dictionary can stand: "a type of producing organization wherein one company prepares several plays, operas, etc., *and produces them alternatively*" (italics mine). Under this definition, a house where one opera with a single cast and conductor is given a run of performances over a week or two or three, while nothing else is produced, is not a repertory company. Even a house that alternates two operas during that stretch is a repertory company only in a minor way. (The system of single-cast-and-conductor productions is known in operatic circles as "stagione"; and today stagione, in pure or diluted form, is the basis of most opera production throughout the world.)

Yet there is a wider sense to the word "repertory"—a sense that encompasses an overview of operatic history from its beginnings to today, and which can be evidenced in a company on the strict stagione system, if that company produces enough operas.

But since it is much harder to grant such an overview if performances do not overlap, most opera houses employ what could be termed a modified stagione system, in which singers, conductors, and even whole casts are replaced during the run of performances.

"Repertory," moreover, can elide into "ensemble opera," which was once its classic definition. One advocate of ensemble opera is Erich Leinsdorf, the respected elder statesman who has been conducting at the Met since 1937. His approach to repertory is simple.

"Repertory is dead as a doornail," he told me. And in his terms it is.

Leinsdorf defines repertory in the European opera-house situation of the nineteenth century, which still existed when he was young in Vienna, and which existed at least partly when he came to the Met.

"You must have a resident company. Without a resident company there is no possibility of any repertory."

By a resident company, Leinsdorf means a largely unchanging group of singers who work in all sorts of operas and thus develop an ensemble operatic sense—"There is no ensemble today, not a trace of it!"—and a continuity.

As part of this company there is a group of four conductors at most: two superior ones and two learned *routiniers* with decades of operatic experience.

"No fledglings who want to show off!"

Given the stability of this arrangement, the opera company can occasionally import a star conductor for a few performances, after which the opera will be taken over by one of the *routiniers*.

Leinsdorf's ideal repertory company would have only two stage directors and a consistent production concept.

Leinsdorf views the current stagione system as an artistic compromise that works against his idea of the repertory system.

"Trans-Atlantic flight was the moment when the whole thing broke down. Now, you can only do modified stagione, and stagione does not appeal to the repeater public, which is the opera public.

That public wants to see *L'amico Fritz* maybe four or five times, but not in two or three weeks. They will come back over a season. But with stagione the opera is gone from the repertory. If opera is compressed into three weeks, it loses its public."

It is an open question whether Leinsdorf's ideal was ever operative at the Met. Certainly in the old days singers traveled less, and there was a greater sense of "company" than today—at least as concerns the stars as opposed to the regulars (the singers of smaller roles, the chorus, and the orchestra). But does this translate into the type of opera Leinsdorf admires? A piece of evidence such as the Met recording of *Carmen* with Rosa Ponselle (recorded on tour in Cleveland in 1937 and recently released in the Met's Historic Broadcast series) quite clearly reveals glaring deficiencies in ensemble, casting, and performance that cannot be written off completely as a substandard "tour performance." Conrad L. Osborne, reviewing the recording in *High Fidelity*, said: "Musically, stylistically and linguistically it is a thorough-going horror that even we who plug for the bad old days could hardly defend, and except for its two principals, its cast does not surpass those that were to be heard on many a night from the barnstorming troupes of Charles Wagner or Fortune Gallo."*

To an extent, of course, Leinsdorf is right: the airplane has changed repertory and performance. But other factors are similarly involved: the greater number of opera performances, the increased demand for star singers—and the money needed to pay them. The whole business of opera has become much more complex, and it is with this business that the Metropolitan Opera must compete, not only as a repertory company but as an artistic enterprise.

These pages will detail one season's responses to the questions posed by this situation. And though they will not resolve questions of what repertory opera should consist of, or whether the Met has

---

*The entire review is worth reading, and can be found in *High Fidelity*, March 1980, pp. 75–77, and in *Records in Review, 1981 Edition* (Great Barrington, Mass.), pp. 67–70.

become, even peripherally, part of New York's intellectual life, they will detail the manifold ways in which New York's other Met museum has faced the challenge of presenting its wares to the public in the later twentieth century.

The exact point at which a Metropolitan Opera season begins is uncertain, but it is definitely not on opening night. With the growth and popularity of opera companies over the past thirty years, both in the United States and throughout Europe, it has become a necessity to plan repertory and to hire singers, conductors, stage directors, and designers further and further in advance. What was once planned two seasons ahead now takes three or four years, and sometimes longer, to arrive at performed fruition.

What occurs is a piecemeal fitting-together, over a span of months and years, of the disparate parts of a repertory season, which at the Met involves seven performances a week (two on Saturday; the house is dark on Sunday). It involves, first, the choosing of new productions (either new settings of repertory works or the introduction of unfamiliar operas—usually from the past—into the repertory), then the signing of casts and conductors, and decisions as to which of the current season's productions will be retained and which will be reintroduced after a hiatus of one season or more.

The pieces of the puzzle come together slowly and with numerous changes along the way. The difficulties presented by the union lockout and subsequent suspension of performances at the beginning of the 1980–81 season only complicated this already fearsome task of scheduling. Although the first task after the settlement of contracts was to provide a curtailed and makeshift season and to plan the annual spring tour, the company very soon had to address itself to 1981–82: what could be salvaged, and what had to be modified or eliminated. This situation kept the specifics of the season in flux well into the spring of 1981—much later than usual—and even necessitated an April announcement of a change of opera from what had already been planned. The always ambitious project of presenting Wagner's complete *Ring* cycle, scheduled for 1981–82, was early reduced to three operas because of

7

lack of rehearsal time and shortage of singers, and this eleventh-hour change reduced the tally to two.

In 1979 the management had announced its plans for four seasons in advance. Some of these plans have already been changed. To a greater extent than ever before, any such scheduling depends on careful allocation of rehearsal time and a balancing of repertory in keeping with higher performance standards as well as a tightened budget.

The extraordinary complexity of these arrangements, in a house that performs seven times a week over a thirty-week season, can only be sketched. There are questions of repertory: As much as possible, the choral burden must be evenly distributed over the season's length. All the new productions must be heard on the Saturday-afternoon Texaco broadcasts, which do not begin until December, when the season is over two months old. There are problems of singer availability. Today, leading singers must be booked years in advance, with little regard to a singer's possible vocal state or his or her aptitude for a role at the time of performance. And singers need to rest between performances, so that a *Tosca* and *Trovatore* with the same prima donna or tenor cannot be scheduled back to back.

Added to this are the problems of scheduling for an audience that is 60 percent a subscription audience. These subscribers, who hear seven or eight performances in a single subscription series, must be given as varied a repertory as possible, with no repeats and with at least one new production included. And this planning extends beyond a single season, for longtime subscribers to, say, a Monday-night series will not welcome hearing much the same repertory that they heard the year before. In the 1981–82 season, all "full" subscriptions included at least one new production, including the two new "German" series, created to appeal to operagoers who would rather hear Wagner than Verdi.

This situation is unique to the Met, which, because it is not state supported, is heavily dependent on subscribers. But the mind-boggling intricacies of this system must be mastered if the Met wishes to stay in business in its present form, since it cannot cancel and reschedule performances, as do many European opera houses.

In the days before the ubiquity of the phonograph record, companies like the Met sought the widest repertory possible, often for only a few performances of each work, which were usually under-rehearsed as far as orchestra, chorus, and minor singers were concerned. The object was to hear the stars and to hear the opera, usually in that order. In both the 1906–07 and the 1912–13 seasons at the Met, to take two examples, eleven operas were played within a two-week period (in 1906–07 there were eleven performances; in 1912–13 there were twelve—one opera, *Madama Butterfly*, was repeated).*

Today, because of casting necessities, operas are given over a span of a few weeks (three to five weeks is normal), and within that span four or five operas alternate performances. The stagione concept has taken hold everywhere, for economic reasons (less time spent in working new singers into roles) and for the obvious advantages of ensemble cohesiveness and (for new productions especially) maintenance of directorial control. In an age dominated by the stage director, this last has become very important.

A repertory theater should be the vision of a single artistic mind (or a group of like-minded individuals) if it is to have a guiding purpose. Since opera as a defined art form has an almost four-hundred-year history, it is incumbent upon an international repertory house to present as much an overview of opera history as possible, if not in one year's repertory, then in a span of three or four years. And if this is a legitimate aim, then the Met stands alone among American opera companies in its ability to fulfill it (and, it may be added, alone among theatrical companies of any sort).

This "museum function" is integral to the Met (as it is to all

---

*In 1906–07, the weeks of December 31 and January 7 featured: *Faust, Hänsel und Gretel, Tosca, Fedora, Lakmé, Siegfried, Lucia di Lammermoor, Roméo et Juliette, L'Africaine, Lohengrin,* and *La Damnation de Faust.* In 1912–13, the weeks of December 30 and January 6 featured: *Tristan und Isolde, Madama Butterfly, Parsifal, Il barbiere di Siviglia, Les Huguenots, Il trovatore, Tosca, Otello, La fanciulla del West, Die Zauberflöte,* and *Les Contes d'Hoffmann.* (In this two-week period, *Tristan, Butterfly, Tosca, Otello,* and *Fanciulla* were all conducted by Toscanini.)

major opera houses), and has been from its inception. Not surprisingly, the bulk of attention has been given to the operas of the nineteenth and the early twentieth century, plus Mozart. The 1981–82 season is a conservative one even by Met standards, with three new productions of extremely popular operas (*La Bohème, Il barbiere di Siviglia,* and *Les Contes d'Hoffmann*) and one of a Mozart masterpiece, *Così fan tutte.* But if one sticks to the central core of opera in performance—the works from Mozart through Puccini's *Turandot* (1926)—the overview can be judged from two points of view: that of the major opera composers and that of the national schools of opera. Here it is instructive to examine the Met's repertory.

I have chosen three seasons for comparison, 1978–79, 1979–80, and 1981–82, since the 1980–81 season was curtailed by the lockout. In those three seasons, as in all others, the bulk of the repertory lay in the nineteenth century; no opera before Mozart was performed. Mozart himself was represented by only three operas (*Die Zauberflöte, Die Entführung aus dem Serail,* and *Così*). Bel canto was represented by the lighter Donizetti (*L'elisir d'amore* and *Don Pasquale*), Bellini's *Norma,* and Rossini's *Barbiere.* By comparison, the later nineteenth-century giants—Verdi and Wagner—and the transcentury one—Puccini—were strongly represented. Verdi had all his middle and late operas with the exception of *La forza del destino, Simon Boccanegra,* and *Falstaff* performed (nine, with *Luisa Miller* the earliest). Wagner had most of his mature work done (six operas), with the exception of two *Ring* operas, *Die Meistersinger,* and *Tristan und Isolde* (performed in the abbreviated 1980–81 season). Puccini had all his major works performed (seven operas, including the three one-acters that make up *Il trittico*) with the exception of *Turandot* (scheduled for 1980–81) and *La fanciulla del West.* The twentieth century's Richard Strauss was represented by three of his four major works (*Elektra, Der Rosenkavalier,* and *Ariadne auf Naxos*) and by *Die Frau ohne Schatten*—*Salome* also appeared in the abbreviated season. The major French opera *Carmen* and the major German opera *Fidelio* were both performed.

Among the national schools of opera, the German and Italian

dominated, with the French, as is commonplace almost everywhere in the operatic world (even in Paris), lagging well behind. The Russian school, never well represented at the Met, was evidenced by Tchaikovsky's *Eugene Onegin* (*Pique Dame* was scheduled but scrubbed), though not by *Boris Godunov*, last given in 1977–78.

If this overview is extended backward for a ten-year span, however, most of the lacunae among nineteenth- and early-twentieth-century operas are filled in, so that a Met operagoer over that time span was able to see the pith of what could be termed the core repertory.

The repertory can be looked at in another way. The operas most performed at the Met are not necessarily the best, but they are a good indication of popular taste over almost a century, include some of the greatest operas written, and in general gibe with the "most performed" lists of opera houses in Europe. Of the list of the twenty-five most-performed operas at the Met through the 1976–77 season, the three years under consideration saw performances of seventeen (68 percent), and the ten-year cycle included them all. If the list is extended to the top fifty operas, the three years include thirty-two (64 percent), and the ten-year span includes all but Massenet's *Manon* (never performed by the Met at Lincoln Center).*

One thing this means is that although the Met now schedules twenty-three to twenty-six operas a year (some in double and triple bills), it owns the sets and costumes for many more. Some of these travel around the country on loan (the Chicago Lyric Opera borrowed two Met productions for its 1981 season), but most are in the warehouse, ready for future seasons.

The core repertory has been, and continues to be, well served

---

*In descending order of performance: *Aida, Bohème, Carmen, Traviata, Tosca, Faust, Butterfly, Pagliacci, Rigoletto, Lohengrin, Cavalleria, Tristan, Walküre, Trovatore, Lucia, Meistersinger, Tannhäuser, Don Giovanni, Barbiere, Rosenkavalier, Figaro, Parsifal, Gioconda, Siegfried, Roméo et Juliette, Zauberflöte, Götterdämmerung, Boris, Otello, Manon, Forza, Hänsel, Ballo, Manon Lescaut, Fidelio, Elisir, Andrea Chénier, Samson, Pelléas, Hoffmann, Turandot, Salome, Rheingold, Falstaff, Holländer, Gianni Schicchi, Don Carlo, Norma, Fledermaus,* and *Così.*

at the Met. But this repertory is to a large extent tied to "box office" and does not fully represent the range of operatic history. And here the Met, like other repertory opera houses, has been a prisoner of its own limitations. Areas of operatic history that have been consistently slighted include almost all operas that predate Mozart (no Monteverdi, Handel—until the 1983–84 season—or Rameau opera has ever been done by the Met), much early Verdi, most operas of the bel canto era, nearly all Slavic operas, and, in a separate but linked category, the operas of the twentieth century. These omissions have been to an extent compensated by the fact that there is another repertory opera house, the New York City Opera, across the plaza, which programs a slightly different group of operas.

If the idea of "repertory" were to be extended past the concept of alternating performances and some sort of historic overview, it should include several considerations. One would be the exploration of the less popular repertory, either for operas that deserve to be heard but will never be repertory items or for works that have a special reason for being performed (composers' anniversaries, contemporary works). Many operas will never reach a wide audience, despite their eminence as works of art, and to include them not only gives the season tone and sinew, but may have the serendipitous result of proving popular. In fact, audiences recently have shown a desire to get away from the standard repertory; and many peripheral operas, if well presented, have attracted sold-out houses, both at the Met and elsewhere. If the museum function of the opera company, so often derided, is taken at all seriously by the management, it would include not only the repetition of the core repertory but the illumination of neglected corners of the historical repertory, as art museums regularly do. This need not mean the hyperinflation of the negligible, for such fare as Handel's operas, the tragédies lyriques of Rameau, Gluck's operas other than *Orfeo ed Euridice,* and the fairy-tale operas of Rimsky-Korsakov are all legitimate candidates for repertory for a house with the resources of the Met.

But it is in the area of what could broadly be termed contemporary opera that the repertory house, wedded to a subscription system and dependent on core repertory, is most vulnerable. It should be remembered in this regard that four-fifths of the twentieth century has elapsed, and thus works like Berg's *Wozzeck* (1925) and *Lulu* (1937) are middle-aged and hardly contemporary. The traditional core repertory peters out with *Turandot*, with only a few isolated operas holding the stage for more than a season since then.

Yet in a true repertory house this state of affairs should count for little. One of the tasks of such a house must be to venture beyond the reflection of past greatness in opera to create and sustain an audience and a climate for all works, whether past or present. What is required is a twofold commitment: to place works of known merit into the ongoing repertory for two, three, or more seasons, and to perform new works—either commissioned operas or promising operas less than a decade old. The word "commitment" is used advisedly, for if there is minimal enthusiasm about the very idea of contemporary opera, as compared with a revival of Verdi's *Macbeth*, the chances of its succeeding are materially lessened.

John Dexter, director of production until late 1980, and James Levine, music director, evidenced that commitment in the cases of Weill's *Rise and Fall of the City of Mahagonny*, Berg's *Lulu*, and Poulenc's *Les Dialogues des carmélites*, the last of which is latest in terms of composition (1957). The introduction of commissioned operas, integral to the management's long-term plans, will not bear fruit until after the Centennial season, 1983–84.

Thus the Met, though more open to innovation in terms of sounds peculiar to this century than the house of the Bing years, remains the museum it was earlier. It does not display that openness to contemporary opera that was characteristic of the Met during the regime of Gatti-Casazza, the only time the Met could be termed aware of current (mainstream, at least) operatic developments. The 1981–82 season, deeply conservative, has as its youngest work Stravinsky's *Oedipus Rex* of 1927, which is firmly part of history, both theatrically and musically.

The pressures for conformity in a house the size and complexity of the Met ever militate against novelty—for technical, financial, and artistic reasons. New productions of core operas that have seen years of service tend to supersede new productions of the more out-of-the-way, but still viable, operas of yesterday or today. And there is only so much money available for new productions. An opera company that does not need to present the central core repertory on a continuing basis can take more chances with novelties. The Met is much more restrictive, even under the current management. Moreover, the management has shied away from a possible solution: that of borrowing from other opera companies productions of works that may not succeed on a long-term basis. It prefers to create its own productions for Lincoln Center. Thus, the full range of repertory opera, from Monteverdi's *Orfeo* to last year's successful world premiere, will not be seen at the Met. What will be seen is the central core repertory, slightly augmented.

		S E P T E M B E R				
21	22	23	24	25	26	26
Norma	**Das**	**La traviata**	**Siegfried**	**Norma**	**Das**	**La traviata**
Levine;	**Rheingold**	*Rescigno;*	*Leinsdorf;*	*Levine;*	**Rheingold**	*Rescigno;*
Scotto,	*Leinsdorf;*	*Malfitano,*	*Payer,*	*Scotto,*	*Leinsdorf;*	*Malfitano,*
Troyanos,	*Shade,*	*Ciannella,*	*Taillon,*	*Troyanos,*	*Shade,*	*Ciannella,*
Domingo,	*Randova,*	*MacNeil*	*Jung,*	*Domingo,*	*Randova,*	*Ellis*
Giaiotti	*Finnilä,*		*Zednik,*	*Giaiotti*	*Finnilä,*	
	Zednik,		*McIntyre/*		*Zednik,*	
	Brenneis,		*Nentwig,*		*Brenneis,*	
	Ulfung,		*Mazura*		*Ulfung,*	
	Nentwig,				*Nentwig,*	
	Mazura,				*Mazura,*	
	Macurdy,				*Macurdy,*	
	Haugland				*Haugland*	

Singing

O pera is singing. Today, opera may be something other than pure singing: the conductor, the director, or even (as we shall see) the stage designer may be the star. But at base, finally, opera is singing—the human voice, free of amplification and developed to its full potential. For most of its almost four-hundred-year life, opera has been singing; and its devotees are in the opera house night after night precisely because the work onstage is being sung. At the Met—though this too is changing—the emphasis has always been on the voices.

This emphasis is perhaps not as evident nowadays as it was in the past, and it was scarcely evident in the casts of the first week of performances of the 1981–82 season. After opening night, those casts did not list the names of singers recognizable by the casual (as opposed to the inveterate) operagoer. Who were Giuliano Ciannella, Gerd Brenneis, Eva Randova, Elisabeth Payer, or Jocelyne Taillon? Katia Ricciarelli, who was scheduled for Violetta in *La traviata,* had already canceled, as had Renato Bruson and Roberta Knie; all three had been replaced. The glittering casts of Wagner operas of the past (or at least of *memories* of Wagner operas of the past) were hardly duplicated by the two *Ring* operas presented the first week. Aside from the conductor, Erich Leinsdorf, only opera buffs would recognize the names of the singers.

Historically, opera has been dominated by the word, or by spectacle, or by music drama; but for most of its career it has existed because of singing—and, strictly speaking, not all the singing, but the singing of those in the leading roles. In the opera seria of the eighteenth century, the audiences quieted only when the castrati began to sing their arias; the recitative—the important connective dialogue—was often drowned by conversation. The operatic output of the nineteenth century was smaller than that of the eighteenth, but it produced most of the operas we see and hear today, and with them it produced a parade of singers, for whom these operas were written and whose voices made the operas famous.

Singing was at the core of the Metropolitan Opera from the start, and was given its indelible historical imprimatur by the presence of Enrico Caruso, a fixture in the house from 1903 to 1920, in which time he gave 626 performances (plus 235 on tour) of 37 roles. The ghost of Caruso hovers as symbol for the multitude of singers who have electrified the audiences at the Met. Those impresarios who have sought to right the balance between "star" singing and ensemble opera—that is, a generative coordination among singing, acting, direction, decor, and orchestra—have found the task rendered more difficult at the Met by the constant pressure to plan in terms of singers rather than anything else. Who is singing this year, who is not; who should be, who should not: these are the questions asked not only by the standees but by the board members, the subscribers, and the media.

Yet despite the inordinate publicity given the handful of "star" singers and their latter-day (but less powerful) counterparts the "star" conductors, their importance over a thirty-week, seven-performance-a-week season has been exaggerated. A goodly percentage of the opera house on almost every night is presold to subscribers, who cannot expect to hear the stars more than occasionally; and if a star does shine, he or she is not likely to be surrounded by other stars, as in the halcyon days of the general managership of Maurice Grau. Increasingly often, operas have succeeded at the Met, artistically and at the box office, as ensemble productions or visual extravaganzas rather than vehicles for stars.

The fact is, however, that if the elite sing few performances over the span of a season, they do contribute to the tone of the season; and it is the many singers who cling to the rungs below the top who carry on the tradition of the Met as a singers' house. These can be up-and-coming artists, singers making their debuts, or those who do the job unspectacularly but well year after year.

This is one of the secrets of the strength of opera as an art form. In a repertory house such as the Met, central core operas will have to be repeated (and repeated and repeated), and thus the chance is given to hear a variety of approaches to a role, or a variety of vocal combinations. The ubiquitousness today of the stagione system—and, more particularly, the current vogue for a director's often idiosyncratic vision of an opera—has inhibited this individual singing and acting freedom. But rightly or wrongly, the Met has experienced this development only in a modified form.

Yet it is true that, even so, the days when a singer of the caliber of tenor Franco Corelli debuted (in the celebrated "double debut" night with Leontyne Price in *Il trovatore*, January 27, 1961) and in the course of the next three seasons sang ten leading roles in the house and two more on tour—those days are gone forever. For the opera buff, who has always been primarily interested in the voice, this was heaven. Today, such a close examination of a singer's potential and realization in a variety of roles can no longer be made, except on records (and that, of course, can be only partly satisfying), or over a decade or more of performances. And by that time, who knows what will have happened to the voice?

This variety, moreover, even in its more limited form today, sets opera and its repertory apart from the spoken theater, especially in the United States. If we have superior actors—actors who are not drawn away from the classics of the theater by the lure of the far more remunerative movies, television series, or even commercials—where can we see them hone their craft on Shakespeare, Ibsen, Shaw, Chekhov, Brecht, Marlowe, or O'Neill?

This is one reason why opera, that supposedly "exotick" form, remains viable. Another, and one appreciated by all who are captivated by it, is paradoxical: the near impossibility of its ideal realization. Opera—that compound of singing, acting, stage design, often ballet, always orchestra—can go wrong a thousand ways each night. One may go to Wilde's *The Importance of Being Earnest* and feel that the ideal was touched; one might see *La Bohème* and feel that the ideal was approached and at times achieved. But one can spend a lifetime of disappointments at *Tristan und Isolde* or *Don Carlos* or *Carmen* and willingly come back again, for the ideal attracts. And even if a performance does touch the ideal, that in no way diminishes the subsequent quest. Peter Pears created Britten's *Peter Grimes*, which was written for his voice, and for almost two decades he *was* the role. Yet Jon Vickers demonstrated that Pears's conception was not the only one possible. Who is the reigning Otello: James McCracken, Carlo Cossutta, Jon Vickers, or Placido Domingo, all of whom bring different qualities to the Moor? Was Kirsten Flagstad the greatest Isolde of our times, or was Birgit Nilsson? (Or was Astrid Varnay, or Frida Leider?) Was Flagstad the greatest Isolde, but Nilsson the greatest Brünnhilde? (Or was Varnay, or was Leider?)

At the Metropolitan Opera, opening nights have traditionally been less the province of the composer or of the conductor than that of the singer. Occasionally, other factors take precedence, usually at the beginning of a general managership, such as Gatti-Casazza's *Aida* in 1908 (a combination of opera, a glittering ensemble of singers, and Toscanini in the pit), Bing's *Don Carlo* in 1950 (an unfamiliar work that set the tone for Bing's regime), or Goeran Gentele's atypical production of *Carmen*, posthumously realized by Bodo Igesz in 1972. Normally, however, the choice of opera is made to showcase a singer. Although that assignment is subject to in-house politics and must be deftly handled so as not to offend, the importance of appearing on opening night is overvalued. In the last twenty years (since the 1961–62 season, and omitting the nonoperatic 1980 opening) Renata Tebaldi appeared once (and only once before that), as did Sutherland, Sills, Caballé, Pavarotti, and Nilsson—and Nilsson sang *Aida,* a role she did not undertake often, and well outside her usual Wagnerian repertory. Of major singers, Placido Domingo and Robert Merrill each sang five, while Leontyne Price's three included the ill-fated new-house première of *Antony and Cleopatra.* Enrico Caruso's record of seventeen out of eighteen—fourteen in a row—seems safe.

If opening night is still somewhat special—sold out to a non-subscription audience at inflated prices ($150 for the most expensive seat in 1981)—it does not have either the attraction or the resultant society high jinks it once did. For one thing, the season begins earlier, in late September rather than in November, when summer is not yet quite over.

The Metropolitan Opera House on Monday, September 21— the house always opens on a Monday—was decked in foliage, and four trumpeters blew fanfares as the crowd entered. That crowd was hardly dressed to kill: many in tuxedos, a few stubbornly in white tie and tails, several in outlandish garb, and the women soignée but not showy. Many business suits, sports jackets, even shirts and jeans. The only high jinks came from a claque: normal procedure when the media are in attendance.

"It's Scotto's show this year," said one inveterate standee, blithely neglecting to mention that other prominent singers (notably Placido Domingo) were involved, and that "Scotto's show" is often called Bellini's *Norma.*

Now, *Norma,* premiered in 1831, is perhaps the most taxing bel canto opera, as well as one of the most difficult operas to stage successfully today. Except for a handful of singers, no one can more than roughly approximate the florid vocalism, which must be inextricably wedded to a firm yet pliable musical line. Beyond this, the central role of Norma calls for both dramatic declamation and coloratura fioritura, for exquisite soft singing and diamond-hard rage at full voice, plus a command of acting to make the recitatives expressive and to wrench the hearts of the audience at such moments as when Norma takes up the dagger to kill her children. The elusive ideal is not about to be encountered every night, or even every decade. (In the opinion of most, if Sutherland did best by the strictly vocal requirements, only Callas came close to encompassing the role; and while Callas's best-sung Normas came early on in her career, her best-acted came later, with the voice already in decay.)

But the complexities of the piece do not end with the role of Norma. The tenor role of Pollione is both taxing and thankless, and the mezzo (originally soprano) role of Adalgisa demands a steady, agile voice and an ability to blend with the prima donna to produce some of the loveliest pure singing ever written. And the orchestral writing must be handled with an appreciation of the work's historical placing: before Verdi. Opera buffs frequently note that Toscanini rehearsed the work and then refused to conduct it, ostensibly because his Norma was inadequate; but the definite implication was that the opera is too difficult for repertory performance.

Renata Scotto tried, and her failures were magnified by the occasion of the performance. If the comment heard that the best singing of the evening came with the national anthem—that beloved moment when everyone can sing at the Met—was a manifest example of operatic cattiness, it typified the undercurrent of disappointment. A difficult opera, leadenly ugly sets (refurbished, it was bravely announced, but to little visible effect), routine staging, and less than transcendent vocalism—these do not make for a memorable opening night, even of the circumscribed sort usual today.

The next three nights all launched different operas, two of which had not been in the repertory for some seasons. These were the only evidence of the Met's desire to produce a *Ring* cycle in 1981–82.

Wagner's *Ring* is one of the tests of a genuine operatic repertory company. Such an undertaking today requires exceptional advance planning and careful scheduling. Still, the *Ring* cycle has always been considered a touchstone of the artistic maturity of a company, and it had been an integral part of the Met's history from the time the first cycle was presented there in 1889 up through the 1940s. Whether this should be so is increasingly an open question. The four operas, if given as a cycle and not separately (often, for instance, *Die Walküre* will appear on its own, as, for instance, in San Francisco in 1982), demand a unified production style and rehearsal time best served when the operas are presented in a "festival" setting: that is, on their own, divorced from the subscription repertory. Covent Garden presents them this way, as does the annual Seattle festival.

The Met has not divorced the operas from their subscription setting, and has shown little inclination to do so beyond creating a non-subscription cycle for those who want only the *Ring*. In addition, the Met, like any major house, is subject to considerations that apply less rigorously to Seattle: that is, the quality of the singers. It is a commonplace to say that there are no Wagner singers left. Whether there were ever more than a few is another open question, because in this context "Wagner singers" means not the smaller roles, but Brünnhilde, Siegfried, and Wotan. And at the Met, these singers are judged less by their acting or characterizational abilities than by sheer vocal power. The kind of Brünnhilde represented by the aforementioned Varnay—or, more to the point, by Gertrud Kappel—will not do: it's Flagstad, Nilsson, Traubel, or nothing. And that limits the field.

In recent years, worldwide if not at the Met, the lack of such voices has been offset either by the "production concept" of a single dictatorial director or by a conductor's wizardry. It is easier to forget the deficiencies of singer X or Y when the focus is on Patrice Chéreau's or Joachim Herz's staging, which totally involves one in loving or hating what is going on, not what is being sung. Similarly, it is easier to respond to the cycle as a unity when it is shaped by a major Wagnerian conductor, such as Reginald Goodall for the English National Opera, or Wilhelm Furtwängler (heard on disc in two cycles, one from La Scala and one from Rome).

The Met, even had it been able to present the cycle complete (it was the chief casualty of the labor difficulties of 1980), could not have competed on those terms, for its production of the *Ring* dates back to 1968, when Herbert von Karajan was persuaded by Rudolf Bing to stage and conduct his Salzburg production in New York. Karajan lasted for the first two operas of the cycle; his visual and directorial concept, by any standards inferior to his aural one, is the Met's continuing legacy. The two operas presented this season, *Rheingold* and *Siegfried,* were cleanly staged by Karajan's assistant Wolfgang Weber. Erich Leinsdorf, the conductor, is solid and thorough, with much Wagnerian experience; but in operatic terms he is a superior example of the Kapellmeister, meaning that there will be no untoward gaffes or lapses, that performances will be fully professional, but that few insights into the work at hand will be afforded.

This situation places the weight squarely back on the singers. And although the Met cast the minor roles strongly, which worked to advantage in an opera like *Rheingold,* which does not depend on the clarion voice, it became more of a problem in the long stretches of *Siegfried.* Manfred Jung is a decent-looking Siegfried, but he gets through the evening by husbanding his smallish voice—as he must, since at the opera's close he meets a fresh-voiced soprano for a twenty-minute duet. The Wotan of the evening, Donald McIntyre, seemed also small-scale in his approach, which was soon explained by an announcement that he was vocally indisposed and had to quit after two acts.

This in turn pointed up a special problem the Met faces with Wagner operas: the need for specialized casts. Wagner singers tend to be confined to that type of opera, outside Germany at least, and the Met has to have substitutes ready to go into the taxing roles immediately. This leads to Wagner being performed in ghetto pockets during the season, and artists spending weeks in hotel rooms waiting to be summoned. Thus, the "other" Wotan, Franz Ferdinand Nentwig, who had two days previously appeared in *Rheingold,* finished *Siegfried.* The exigencies of the subscription system demand this cover casting, which adds to the cost of opera, for the Met cannot, as some European houses do, postpone or cancel a performance, and only as a last resort will it substitute one opera for another. In Europe, where replacements are within an hour's flying time, this is less of a problem.

The cover casting has its advantages, since often the first cover artist (the Met also has second and third covers for certain roles) is given a couple of performances; thus, if he or she has some particular individuality, it can be heard and seen. For instance, two superior but light-voiced tenors, Ragnar Ulfung and Heinz Zednik, alternated the roles of Mime and Loge.

Even so, the questions remain. Is it the duty of a major repertory house to present revivals of standard operas when the singers are not available? Or should the operas be retired until and unless the opera can be cast, conducted, or directed in an arresting way? If the latter course is taken, as it may be with out-of-the-way works like *Adriana Lecouvreur* or *Semiramide* or *Thaïs,* there will be gaps in the repertory—particularly in the Wagner canon. The question is, in fact, one of the unanswerable ones that enliven the performance of opera with controversy, for one person's cherished memory is another's forgettable clod, for a variety of reasons; and those who choose singers are not necessarily more knowledgeable by virtue of their titles than those who listen. Yet that question was immediately posed by the opening week's *Norma* and *Siegfried.* The Met remains steadfastly committed to the core repertory, with its idea of the best casts available, and in so doing it will continue to draw fire on this precise point.

S E P T E M B E R / O C T O B E R						
28	29	30	1	2	3	3
Madama Butterfly	**Siegfried**	**Norma**	**La traviata**	**Siegfried**	**Norma**	**Das Rheingold**
Fulton;	*Leinsdorf;*	*Levine;*	*Rescigno;*	*Leinsdorf;*	*Levine;*	*Leinsdorf;*
Cruz-Romo,	*Payer,*	*Scotto,*	*Malfitano,*	*Payer,*	*Scotto,*	*Shade,*
Bybee,	*Taillon,*	*Troyanos,*	*Ciannella,*	*Finnilä,*	*Troyanos,*	*Randova,*
Moldoveanu,	*Jung,*	*Domingo,*	*Ellis*	*Jung,*	*Domingo,*	*Taillon,*
Thompson	*Zednik,*	*Giaiotti*		*Ulfung,*	*Giaiotti*	*Zednik,*
	Nentwig,			*McIntyre,*		*Jenkins,*
	Mazura			*Mazura*		*Ulfung,*
						Nentwig,
						Dene,
						Macurdy,
						Haugland

Singing Plus

The fourth opera presented during the first week (repeated in the second) and the opera that led off that second week of repertory were both standard core works: Verdi's *La traviata* and Puccini's *Madama Butterfly*. *La traviata* was the last new production of the abbreviated 1980–81 season (March 17), and the cast on September 23 was not the one that had performed at the premiere, but one that performed the opera later, on the spring tour. Thus, the cast, chorus, and orchestra were thoroughly rehearsed in the production—an important factor at the beginning of a season, when a number of works vie for rehearsal attention. The Met under its current management does not like to offer new productions until well into the season (no management likes to offer them on opening nights), because of the rehearsal time involved. And it should be remembered that staging, singing, and orchestral rehearsals are not the only ones. Lighting rehearsals are extremely time consuming, and require the sets to be onstage, which means that the stage is pre-empted. Already in the first weeks, some of the settings for December's Stravinsky trio and new *La Bohème* were onstage to be assembled and lit.

September's Violetta was the young American soprano Catherine Malfitano, whose father plays second violin in the Met orchestra. One of the continual complaints about the Met—it was virulent in Bing's days—is that the house rarely develops singers, and usually signs them after the peak of their careers. As is the rule with most generalizations, the charge is only partly true; it can be refuted as easily as evidenced. The Met has always maintained—or at least left it open to inference—that it is the Academy of singing, and that a singer must therefore be nominated several times and tested before entrance. But this is largely pose. When Nilsson debuted in 1959, she was at the height of her powers; when Sylvia Sass, a not ungifted soprano, debuted in a difficult role, it was evident that she was not ready to appear as Tosca at the Met. The opportunity to nurse along a singer who may become a star through a few seasons of lesser roles, as Covent Garden did with Joan Sutherland, is increasingly jeopardized by the lure of big roles and big money elsewhere, or by the singers' (or their managers') idea of what their careers should be. In a media showcase like the Met, it is difficult to hide real talent, and opera companies throughout the United States and abroad are hungry enough, and have enough money, to provide irresistible temptations.

Malfitano, of course, arrived at the Met well prepared (as most American singers are today), not only in the intricacies of opera but in the particular role of Violetta. Violetta is one of the plum roles for soprano: it is immensely appealing to an audience as well as vocally gratifying. Yet, like Norma, it is not just one kind of singing. It requires coloratura and lyricism in the first act, and the feeling of awakened love, and demands a developed dramatic ability in the second and last acts. The central scene with Alfredo's father, in which Violetta is convinced that her liaison must be sacrificed for the good of her lover's family, requires a very different temperament from that which tosses off Act I. Thus, there are lyric Violettas, nightingale Violettas, and dramatic Violettas, but seldom equally in one singer. Additionally, at the Met even more than at other opera houses, all Violettas are scrutinized not only through the microscope of the present but through the microscope of the past.

This is doubtless unfair. No artist should be forced to compete with ghosts. Yet the Met, as a court of last resort and as a historical entity, imposes that sense of history on all major artists, both by the weight of its past achievements and, more immediately, by the press releases and the notes carried in the program. The notes for *Traviata* list over twenty previous Met Violettas.

Further, any new Violetta will be judged against recordings of the great Violettas, past and present, not only complete recordings but versions of individual arias. An opera buff will be able to compare a dozen renditions of "Ah! fors' è lui" and "Sempre libera" for various vocal factors, and at least some of that knowledge rings in the ears when any new artist is heard. Malfitano therefore faced a far more daunting task than when she appeared, in the spring of 1981, as Thérèse in Poulenc's *Les Mamelles de Tirésias*. Then, only a very few had seen or heard the artist who created the role and who was Poulenc's favorite female singer, Denise Duval.

Malfitano brought to the role the strengths of an American singer: an appealing figure and onstage presence, an intense musicality, and a youthful, fresh voice that could handle the requirements. She was comfortable onstage, but more, she was alive vocally and physically. If Malfitano cannot yet challenge the role's finalists, in the words of a respected opera impresario "she picks up her check"—which many artists do in fact, but not in any artistic sense. And while watching her Violetta, I was conscious of the work she and her tenor, Giuliano Ciannella, had put into the performance during the spring tour performances.

There are certain moments apart from the vocal ones that are always used as touchstones for Violetta. One of them is how the soprano handles the great "Amami, Alfredo!" passage, when Violetta, about to leave Alfredo, pours out her heart in a final farewell. Malfitano's stage movements no less than her vocalism told me that we were in the presence of a singing actress, an up-and-coming soprano perfecting her art. The other aspects of the evening receded: this alone was worth the attendance.

Madama Butterfly is the Met's quintessential repertory work. Its setting, by Japanese designer Motohiro Nagasaka, was once exquisitely beautiful, but by now it has been refurbished and repainted so often that it has become garish in its obviousness. (It dates back to 1958, making it one of the Met's oldest productions in terms of service; the company's *Don Giovanni* and *Eugene Onegin* are older, but neither has seen comparable use.) The opera therefore becomes a repertory filler: something that attracts subscribers (who have tickets anyway), casual visitors who want to see the inside of the Met and those who want "easy opera," and the one or two who are fans of the leading lady. The leading lady on the first night was a dependable house artist, the Mexican soprano Gilda Cruz-Romo, but what was immediately evident was not the fact that she had a cold (announced in the second intermission), but that she was visually unsuited for the role.

The hoariest of clichés about opera is the vision of the huge woman in breastplate and wingèd helmet, howling out music; the hoariest of attacks on the form is that "the singers are fat and don't know how to act." In recent years, certainly, singers have taken off weight (the most notable instance being Maria Callas, and you can easily find someone to state that her vocal troubles got worse the slimmer she got). But the very nature of the art requires lots of breath and lots of stamina, and that is equated with heft. Vocal buffs have never worried about physical appearance or even acting, as the career of Montserrat Caballé attests; and latterly the operatic media king, Luciano Pavarotti, for all the publicity given his diets, has made fat fashionable.

But there are roles and roles, and a Cio-Cio-San strains credulity to the limit when she appears looking like a sumo wrestler, nearly as tall as her American naval lieutenant paramour—and let's ignore the fact that she's supposed to be fifteen. Cruz-Romo can get away with her appearance in the middle operas of Verdi, but the verismo works of Puccini require figure as well as voice—unless a singer's voice can do 90 percent of the job required. In a work based on the strict fidelity to "real life" of David Belasco's fantasy about Japan, Cruz-Romo was miscast, surrounded by nice American men and women in costume; and her always superficial garnishes of how to play a Japanese maiden (there probably are books for sopranos on this) contrasted unfavorably with the inner conviction of Malfitano's Violetta.

The house emptied fast at the end; the subscribers headed home without acknowledging that the soprano had managed her voice well enough to get through the death scene without catastrophe. Perhaps the anodyne of the announcement ameliorated her cold, at least for the evening.

			O C T O B E R			
5	6	7	8	9	10	10
La traviata	**Norma**	**Madama**	**Das**	**Siegfried**	**Madama**	**La traviata**
Rescigno;	*Levine;*	**Butterfly**	**Rheingold**	*Leinsdorf;*	**Butterfly**	*Rescigno;*
Malfitano,	*Scotto,*	*Fulton;*	*Leinsdorf;*	*Payer,*	*Fulton;*	*Malfitano,*
Ciannella,	*Troyanos,*	*Cruz-Romo,*	*Shade,*	*Taillon,*	*Cruz-Romo,*	*Ciannella,*
MacNeil	*Domingo,*	*Bybee,*	*Randova,*	*Jung,*	*Bybee,*	*MacNeil*
	Giaiotti	*Moldoveanu,*	*Finnilä,*	*Ulfung,*	*Moldoveanu,*	
		Thompson	*Zednik,*	*McIntyre,*	*Thompson*	
			Jenkins,	*Dene*		
			Ulfung,			
			McIntyre,			
			Mazura,			
			Macurdy,			
			Haugland			

Subscriptions, Subscribers, and Supporters

The third week of repertory saw but repeats of previously presented operas; all were subscription performances. The subscription system is the basis for the Met's repertory and, indeed, for its existence, for it is the subscribers who, along with the patrons of the opera, form the backbone of the finances of the company, through both their ticket purchases and their donations.

The subscription system is endemic to all American performing arts (even new-music series have subscriptions), and its value is such that its use is growing in Europe, the bastion of state-supported art. The attraction of the subscription system is not so much that it guarantees audience as that it guarantees income. Subscribers are required to rehire their seats for the coming season by June, with full payment due then; and though this money cannot legally be spent until the performances take place, it can and does earn interest while it is lying supposedly fallow—and recent interest rates have been at levels once considered usurious.

Since subscriber monies, as we shall see, total well over $10 million, it is not surprising that subscribers are actively sought, and that they are cosseted as "members of the Met family," a selling device to confer an aura of exclusivity and preference.

This subscriber domination was, of course, always the case, and far more so in days past. Even after the heyday of the Golden Horseshoe—that expanse of private boxes that excluded the socially unwashed (Jews, even Otto Kahn, need not apply)—and the tradition that only Monday-night subscribers (the classiest crowd) were allowed to buy tickets for opening night (Bing abrogated that privilege), the Met quite consciously displayed to the city and the country the attitude of a closed corporation. The Depression, which brought acres of empty seats and the near bankruptcy of the company, loosened these traditions through the efforts of Mrs. August Belmont, the creation of the Metropolitan Opera Guild, and the national broadcasts and appeals for funds. But even in the 1950s, under Rudolf Bing, the shorter seasons were from 70 to 80 percent subscribed. It was difficult to get tickets unless you knew a ticket broker or a subscriber or were an opera buff, for schedules were rarely published more than ten days in advance, and tickets for, say, a *Bohème* were sold only for the next performance or two, never for one a month away. The Met's advertising budget was minuscule: small tombstone ads listing at most the next week's operas, usually followed by the words "sold out."

All of this changed because of union contracts that guaranteed payment over an increasing number of weeks. That meant longer seasons and more performances—and higher ticket prices—and in turn necessitated more and shorter subscription series. There was also the general reaction of "If they don't want me, I don't want them" of prospective non-subscription ticket buyers. The emergence of competing attractions—especially television—the flight to the suburbs, the dying out of older, loyal subscribers: all meant fewer seats sold, and therefore less revenue. The fact that labor contracts now provided a reasonable wage backstage and in the pit, with the concomitant skyrocketing costs of producing an artistic product that must be, in terms of the various factors involved, the most labor-intensive of any art form, only accelerated this financial drain. And so the gap between subscriber revenues and costs grew ever wider. Even if you sold out the house every night, you'd still go bankrupt.

Added to this was the perceived necessity—heretofore thought inconceivably socialistic—of applying for the state and government funds that were slowly becoming available; no single contributor could bail out the company as Otto Kahn had. Clearly, the Met's image had to change.

And it *has* changed—dramatically. What was once a closed corporation now trumpeted ticket availability in newspapers, on radio, and through the mails. You can buy tickets by phone and charge them to your credit card. The notorious "Strike a blow for civilization" campaign—pure Madison Avenue—equated opera at the Met with Culture at its highest. The barbarians would be stopped in their tracks by "Celeste Aida." Marketing opera came into being, and aggressively took a greater and greater share of attention (the marketing department today lists seventeen names in the program, for tickets, promotion, opera shop, subscription, group sales, telephone sales, mail order, and raffle, among others). The Met today, like soap or cars, is sold as a commodity, albeit one wrapped in the glistening package of a civilization enhancer.

The ramifications of this effort circle outward from the subscribers and other blood relations of the Met "family" (patrons, Guild members) to those around the country (in the Met tour cities, or as members of the National Council of the Metropolitan Opera), to the general public in New York and its surrounding suburbs, to visitors from here and abroad, as part of packaged tours or on their own. In this effort the Met is no different from other arts companies around the United States—Glynn Ross's Seattle Opera markets its product even more aggressively. But it differs in that the management constantly stresses the fact that the Met is "our national opera company." In this way it seeks to enshrine its pre-eminence by fiat and to garner supporters for its seasons from every source.

All the names and addresses obtained by this marketing outreach are kept on file and constantly updated. The Met master file now numbers upwards of three-quarters of a million names, and these are used for a variety of mailings throughout the year. For instance, Met raffle tickets were sent across the country, and in 1981 the three top prizes were won by individuals in, respectively, San Diego; Columbia, South Carolina; and Washington, D.C. Of the top fifty winners, only nine were from the boroughs of New York, with nine more from the suburbs.

Yet the subscribers remain the basis on which this edifice is built—and for good reason. They are loyal: the renewal rate is around 80 percent (in 1981 it was a shade higher). And many subscribers are patrons of the opera as well. They regularly give contributions in excess of their annual subscription charge—roughly 20 percent of the subscribers donate the "suggested" added figure—and they buy additional tickets.

Today, the Met claims that it consciously has restricted its subscriptions to a lower percentage than in the past—about 60 percent. It has done this because the management has found that many of its "family" members like to select individual performances outside their subscriptions, and that these tickets might be unavailable if all the best seats were held for subscribers. Since the upper class of family members—the patrons—pay a minimum of $1,500 per year for this privilege of ordering tickets for individual operas (among other privileges), and the patrons in various categories number sixteen hundred, it behooves the house to reserve good tickets for such sales.

For the 1981–82 season, ticket prices were scaled from $45 to $10 Monday through Thursday. Friday and Saturday performances, always in heavy demand, were priced from $55 to $11; and the Christmastime *Hansel and Gretel* ranged from $25 to $10. Center boxes for all but the *Hansels* were $60 a ticket.

Two additional points should be made. One is that the Lincoln Center house was specifically designed by Wallace K. Harrison to accommodate a great number of orchestra seats at top prices, in order to maximize revenue for a full house of 3,800 seats. The second is that 1981–82 prices for Broadway musicals, which are invariably amplified, range downward from a $40 top on week-ends, and even straight plays get $35 a seat. And in 1982 the Santa Fe Opera charged, for a seat in its open-air theater, $32 during the week and $36 on weekends. Prices at European summer festi-vals can be much higher—up to $150 a ticket. One should also remember that in many European opera houses there are two price scales: one (lower) for performances with regular house art-ists and one (higher) for productions involving top stars. Except for certain opening nights, the Met has only one price.

A sold-out house grosses roughly $104,000 on a weekday, and one week of sold-out houses will gross roughly $775,000. Extrap-olated over a thirty-week season, the figure is just in excess of $23 million; and about $12 million of that is generated by subscrip-tions.

The Met, understandably, does not offer many non-subscription performances during the season. In 1981–82, there were a total of sixteen, not including the *Hansel*s: one opening night, two Guild benefits of new productions (a time-honored fund-raising device), two Sunday-evening concerts (made possible by the terms of the new union contracts), and two "events": a Verdi Requiem and a gala evening of opera acts in honor of tenor Carlo Bergonzi. Of the remaining nine "Met family performances" (its appellation) five were on Saturday evening and one on New Year's Eve (another tradition), and they included such crowd-pleasers as *La traviata, La Bohème, Madama Butterfly, Tosca,* and *Rigoletto,* along with (a third tradition) the Good Friday *Parsifal* (it used to be in the afternoon, but is now in the evening). The Met does not tempt box-office fate with non-subscription novelties (last year's *Mahagonny,* inserted for a canceled opera after the labor difficulties, was a box-office disas-ter); the only such concession to adventure was a Saturday-evening performance of *I vespri siciliani,* a seldom-performed Verdi opera.

The Met monitors its ticket sales with extreme care, for if each percentage point of subscription sales is significant, so is every point of total sales. The man in the house with the best track record for nosing out potential in this area is also one of the oldest employees in terms of service: box-office manager Alfred F. Hubay. Hubay began as an usher in the old house in the 1943–44 season and has participated in the regimes of general managers from Edward Johnson to Anthony Bliss.

Hubay is an extremely accurate predicter of ticket sales, and his prognosticating abilities have long been known to those interested in that arcane subject. He cheerfully admits when he is wrong, but usually his errors are conservative rather than visionary; and he insists that over a season's span the guesses average out.

One factor in sales is that as a rule the first part of the season (now, with the season beginning earlier, the months of September and October) sells badly, while at the end of the season almost everything sells. (This was one reason why Bing scheduled the new production of Berg's *Wozzeck* for the spring of 1959, and its first revival for the spring of 1961.) But the 1981–82 season has confounded Hubay: ticket sales have been strong from the start, even though the press has turned thumbs down on most of the performances. ("It would be charitable to consider the first three weeks of the Met season as a bad dream," said Leighton Kerner in *The Village Voice* [October 27, 1981].)

"Can you believe," Hubay said, "that the October 3 Saturday of *Norma* and *Rheingold* did $239,000 worth of business? Or that the October 7 performance of *Butterfly*—on the eve of Yom Kippur, always an off night—did 98 percent?"

What is generally true, however, is that a new production of an unfamiliar work will not sell until the reviews are in, and then, if they are favorable, tickets will disappear. This is what happened with the French trio (*Parade*) in 1981, and what the Met hopes will happen with the Stravinsky trio this season. The question mark comes with the revival, especially if there is a lapse of a season in between. Often the current rage becomes the has-been dud. Until the French trio, it was a given in operatic scheduling that, with the obvious exceptions of *Cavalleria rusticana* and *Pagliacci*, one-acters never, but never, sell. Puccini's *Trittico*, meant as a single evening and given its world premiere at the Met, has never done extraordinary business there, no matter what the cast. It is scheduled for the sixth week.

Of course, none of the above impinges, except obliquely, upon artistic merit. But the ring of the cash register does blot out the Bronx cheers, as well as demonstrate that opera, as practiced by the Met, continues to an extent independent from the strictures of the press or of the cognoscenti—at least for central core works. Why the *Butterfly* I saw should prompt over three thousand people to pay to see it (as they did for a non-subscription performance on October 17) remains a mystery, except that the Puccini music was being given in some sort of fashion, unsatisfactory by most standards but apparently enjoyable to those who like the tunes and want to cry discreetly at little Trouble in the arms of his father (not in Puccini, but one of the conceits of this staging), while his mother lies stretched out dead on the tatami.

O C T O B E R

12	13	14	15	16	17	17
Die Frau ohne Schatten *Leinsdorf; Marton, Nilsson, Dunn, Brenneis, Nentwig*	**La traviata** *Rescigno; Malfitano, Ciannella, Ellis*	**Madama Butterfly** *Fulton; Cruz-Romo, Bybee, Alexander, Edwards*	**Siegfried** *Leinsdorf; Yoes, Taillon, Jung, Ulfung, McIntyre, Dene*	**La traviata** *Rescigno; Malfitano, Ciannella, Ellis*	**Die Frau ohne Schatten** *Leinsdorf; Marton, Nilsson, Dunn, Brenneis, Nentwig*	**Madama Butterfly** *Fulton; Cruz-Romo, Bybee, Alexander, Edwards*

Down Memory Lane

Memory is the curse as well as the balm of the operagoer. Indeed, it is memory that gives this art form its particular resonance and addictiveness. Why, otherwise, return for a fiftieth *Tosca*? If for the music, then better to hear a fiftieth *Nozze di Figaro*. If it is in part to revisit old haunts and friends, and to live in a known and definable world, it is also to place an immediate bit of history into the memory book along with all the other bits. In a society wedded to the present, the immediate, and the transitory, the operagoer is an anachronism, like the baseball fan, for the present is lived in company with the past—the past of the listener's experience and the historical past of tradition.

The Grand Game of opera is that of comparisons, and the older the operagoer is, the more fiercely it is played. It is played most compulsively with singers, both singers' live performances of yore and their recorded performances on disc and tape, but it is also played with conductors and with productions. "Yes, but you didn't hear X in the role"; "Of course, but if you haven't seen it in Salzburg, you haven't seen it, period"; "There are no Aidas today" (or Violettas, or Normas, or Siegfrieds). The memory's image hardens to concrete, and rational discussion becomes useless. How can Domingo compare to Gigli, Martinelli, Bjoerling, or Tucker—not to mention the sainted Caruso? The oldest and most encrusted memorists retire from all performances, to live on nostalgia.

Memory, however, plays nefarious tricks. Performances heard in youth, when the opera or the singers are fresh acquaintances, tend to become touchstones.

Memory accretes, from the single performance to the Golden Age. "I remember when Nilsson and Sutherland and Tebaldi and Milanov followed one another at the Met," said one longtime operagoer. "That doesn't happen today!"

And I remember, when all of those were following each other (and Milanov, by the way, singing not so well, in the twilight of her career), listening to someone else say, "Flagstad and Melchior and Tibbett and Ponselle and Rethberg—those were the days!" And on and on, backwards, to the dawn of the yellow-brick brewery on Thirty-ninth Street.

It's a grand game, and it is regularly played in the standing room and in the boxes and across the dinner tables and, always, in print (the annual "Golden Age, Where Art Thou Gone?" Sunday *New York Times* piece for 1981 appeared on October 11). The truly wizened practitioners—the Casey Stengels of the game—eschew the Tuckers and the Corellis, the Warrens and the Merrills, the Albaneses and the de los Angeleses (and conveniently forget the Kurt Baums, the Mary Curtis-Vernas, and the Randolph Symonettes) to concentrate on old records, on the Mapleson cylinders recorded from the flies of the old house, or the baritones who could trill and embellish, or the lone castrato captured in old age for posterity. "Listen to this, with the pitch corrected to play at 73 rpm," etc., etc. . . . and the grand game continues.

Memory, however, can be and is a paradisiacal blessing. One selected night is symbolic. That was the eighth performance of the inaugural season in the Lincoln Center house (October 2, 1966), which happened to be the fourth new production of that season.

The crowd, apart from lovers of the opera on records (it was then rarely staged), did not expect much, being worn out by the preceding week of glories. It was a fairy-tale opera (a genre not often seen at the Met, and never popular) by a composer known for other operas: *Die Frau ohne Schatten*, by Richard Strauss.

The opera has only rarely since played to anything but sold-out houses, with people in the Lincoln Center Plaza up to a block away from the Met imploring extra tickets at whatever price.

This was so in part because of the bravura of the production, for Robert O'Hearn's sets were a fairy-tale wonderland ("over-sugared," said the Curmudgeon). All the wizardry of the Met's stage (save the turntable, wrecked by Zeffirelli's *Antony and Cleopatra* production and only repaired in time for *Frau*'s second revival) was turned loose, so that stages moved up and down, and singers caroled from the roof of the auditorium.

The mandarin aesthete Robert Craft dismissed the memory: "[The Met production] was designed to show off the mechanical resources of the company's new stage. These, at any rate, were the stars of the performance. . . . But the glitter and dazzle only pointed up the threadbare quality of the acting. . . ." (*New York Review of Books*, September 24, 1981) And perhaps his memory coincided with his predispositions, for to those who love the work and returned to hear it again, the stars were not the mechanics but the performances, of the entire cast and especially of three of them, which were anything but threadbare in either acting or acting with the voice: Leonie Rysanek, Walter Berry, and Christa Ludwig. Ludwig, in superior voice, encompassed and defined the role of the Dyer's Wife. One transcendent stage moment burned itself indelibly on the minds of those who chose to see: Lying on the bed from which she has banished her husband, Ludwig as the wife lifted her head and stared out at the audience in a growing realization of the consequences of her act as, in the background, three Watchmen sing in praise of fertility. Berry's natural humanity in this, to many his greatest, role, the grace of his movements, and his wholehearted rough simplicity were at one with Barak, the Dyer. And Rysanek honed her pulsing, thrilling voice to the illuminating climax in the fountain scene when the Empress rejects her own salvation because it is bought at the expense of others. These performances coalesced into glowing memory, encased in a reading of power and sweep by Karl Böhm, who considered himself Strauss's chief disciple and who was until 1981–82 the only conductor to perform the work at the Met.

Die Frau ohne Schatten was not originally scheduled for this season. It became a possibility when *Götterdämmerung* was canceled, since *Frau* could employ many in that cast. And it had the added attractions of being a popular work and of being one of the few roles in Birgit Nilsson's current repertory.

Birgit Nilsson (born in 1918) is now in the final stages of her great opera career and has only recently returned to the Met after an absence prompted by difficulties with the U.S. Internal Revenue Service. Her voice, while still huge and brazen, today takes longer to warm up, so that the pitch is more often insecure and the sound tends to a shrillness. Yet she *is* performing, and is therefore a living memory; and to her countless fans, the remembrance of things past become more controlling than the actual sounds produced. The Metropolitan Opera Guild seized on the occasion of her appearance as the Dyer's Wife to hold its forty-seventh annual luncheon in the grand ballroom of the Waldorf-Astoria in her honor on October 26, and the heartfelt tribute of its welcome and its delineation of her two hundred performances at the Met brought tears to her eyes. "I love you," she said, holding her gift ceramic (New York) apple. The overflow of nostalgia engulfed the pencil-slim figure of Sir Rudolf Bing as well; as he received the second-biggest ovation of the afternoon, *una furtiva lagrima* could be noted on the cheek of that normally reserved and austere patrician.

For this *Frau,* however, Karl Böhm was no longer in the pit. His death in August only ratified the change, which would see an almost totally new cast in the opera. But the Met recognized his contribution with a line in the program—"This revival of *Die Frau ohne Schatten* is dedicated to the memory of Karl Böhm"—and a note from the evening's conductor, Erich Leinsdorf.

The cast on October 12 was, as noted, completely different from that of 1966, except for the Second Watchman of Robert Goodloe. But the reception was as enthusiastic as that of the first year, both in the press and with the public. And yet—and yet—if the memory can play tricks, it can also be accurate.

Leaving aside the merits of this cast versus the original one, the focus is on the production, and any production so heavily dependent on visual as well as vocal glitter will fade with time. This is inevitable—especially when, as is the case here, the original creators of the production (O'Hearn and director Nathaniel Merrill) are no longer in charge to restage and refurbish it. The Met keeps elaborate production books, so that the original can be as nearly as possible approximated. But new singers and time's march will marmorealize what once was fresh, and invest with routine what once was spontaneous. For instance, the aforementioned moment of Ludwig staring into the night was duplicated by Nilsson. But Nilsson has never been the actress Ludwig was (and is), and what fit Ludwig's conception does not necessarily fit Nilsson's. The moment passed unnoticed, for to have redirected the scene to take advantage of what Nilsson could offer would have taken too much rehearsal time for such a complicated work.

If the first thing to fail in an aging athlete is his legs, the first thing to go in an opera production is, oddly enough, the lighting. Lighting was once not an important factor in opera production. It was used to show daylight, dawn or dusk, and night, with the ubiquitous follow-spot to highlight whoever was singing. But today, lighting is probably the most important single factor in staging, and in most cases certainly more important than the specifics of the sets. Most of Wieland Wagner's ideas of stage dramatics were expressed through lighting and chiaroscuro, which had to be handled with extreme subtlety. Franco Zeffirelli's notable production of Verdi's *Falstaff* at the Met in 1964 gained immeasurably from his use of lighting—and this in the old house, with its antiquated lighting system which gave Zeffirelli fits. I remember at the time being struck by the change in the lighting during the run after Zeffirelli had left: even though he had given precise directions, the result tended to increasing obviousness and banality. And this happens in the new house, even with its lighting systems programmed: what must be by its very nature evanescent and evocative cannot be computerized.

Robert O'Hearn's sets for *Die Frau ohne Schatten,* like the entire production, were enhanced by his inventive and constantly altering use of the lighting boards in the new house. The magical scene of the Emperor's monologue in Act II, for instance, was played in a dim forest of silvers and bluish greens, stretching out into the darkness like some underwater kingdom.

All of this was gone in 1981, replaced by a stolid lighting plan that may have been based on the original, but that flattened out the depths and made what should have been subtle obvious. What was worse, the lighting illuminated the sets so that instead of seeming like mysterious mirages of a never-never land, they stood revealed in both their tinsel and their piecemeal placing onstage— lumps of sugar surrounded by voids. The magic inherent in *Die Frau ohne Schatten* or in the singers' voices may have still been present, but the magical qualities of the production—so integral to this opera—had vanished. In this instance, it was obvious that O'Hearn's lighting plan had been altered. But in more than one revival I have noticed that the lighting, which should be totally computer programmed and therefore not subject to change from the time it is fixed, has in fact changed, and become less evocative in almost every instance. There remains a distance between a computer and an individual's pair of eyes.

			O C T O B E R			
19	20	21	22	23	24	24
Rigoletto	**Siegfried**	**Madama**	**La traviata**	**Die Frau**	**Rigoletto**	**Madama**
Patanè;	Leinsdorf;	**Butterfly**	Rescigno;	**ohne**	Patanè;	**Butterfly**
Blegen,	Yoes,	Kohn;	Malfitano,	**Schatten**	Blegen,	Kohn;
Jones,	Taillon,	Cruz-Romo,	Ciannella,	Leinsdorf;	Jones,	Cruz-Romo,
Lloveras,	Jung,	Bybee,	Bruson	Marton,	Lloveras,	Bybee,
Manuguerra,	Zednik,	Alexander,		Nilsson,	Manuguerra,	Alexander,
Hines	McIntyre,	Edwards		Dunn,	Hines	Edwards
	Mazura			Brenneis,		
				Nentwig		

Productions

Monday, October 19 saw the season's first performance of Verdi's *Rigoletto*. This production, new in 1977–78, was roughly handled in the press because of the direction of John Dexter and the ugliness of Tanya Moiseiwitsch's unit set. It remains in the repertory, though, because of several factors, the most obvious of which is that *Rigoletto* is a core repertory work: its music and its dramatic punch appeal to a wide audience. The anguish of the jester, the hedonistic cruelty of the Duke, and the lost innocence and martyrdom of the jester's daughter continue to be powerful advocates for the opera. Moreover, two of today's superstar tenors, Placido Domingo and Luciano Pavarotti, have sung the tenor role. (Domingo would not be heard in the opera this season, but Pavarotti would undertake it later on, including a televised performance.)

Until he relinquished the position in 1981, John Dexter was director of production at the Met, which meant that he oversaw the revivals of operas with a view to refurbishing them and stream-lining all sorts of backstage problems of getting operas onstage. He also, of course, provided ideas for future productions, and directed many of them himself. Today, Dexter is still in the house, though on a more limited basis, and he supervised the revival of *Rigoletto* while preparing the new production of Stravinsky works for December.

Although it is generally felt that Dexter brought a consistency of vision to his work, it is also conceded that this vision worked much better for twentieth-century operas than for nineteenth-century classics such as *Rigoletto*. Yet what is finally controlling from an operatic rather than from a Met-eyed point of view is not the various deficiencies of his idea of *Rigoletto*, played for melodrama in a constricting setting either phallic or evocative, for some unknown reason, of the Tower of Babel. What is controlling is that John Dexter came from a background of the spoken theater.

Theater directors working in opera are today commonplace, though thirty years ago Rudolf Bing caused considerable flutter when he hired Margaret Webster, Alfred Lunt, and Tyrone Guthrie to direct at the Met. Up to then, in the United States at least, it was a general assumption that the stage director was someone thoroughly familiar with opera and the specific opera at hand; but he was primarily a "scenic blocker," someone who charts movements—a traffic cop, whose primary duty was to keep the show moving and make sure that the chorus was out of the way of the stars. Theater directors, then and now, seldom had firsthand knowledge of opera, and brought to their tasks a perhaps welcome freshness but also an idiosyncratic point of view.

Yet, since Bing's early years, theater in Europe and even here has moved in new directions at a far more rapid and adventurous pace than opera, so that any self-respecting theater director will today be operating under a differing set of assumptions from those of 1950. And those assumptions will be naturally carried over to opera. Thus, the expanded employment of theater directors in opera has caused what must be termed the single most explosive revolution in opera in recent years. Stage direction—or,

as it is called everywhere but in the United States, "production"—
is today at the very center of operatic performance.

The word "revolution" is used advisedly, for this development
strikes directly at several basic conceptions of what opera is. First
of all, this development is primarily, and in many cases exclusively,
visually oriented. The actual singing, as far as pitch or phrase (not
character portrayal) is concerned, is left untouched, and the composer's *music,* onstage and in the pit, is also unchanged. What is
changed is what the audience sees. Thus, one can arrive at schizo-
phrenic productions like the Nikolaus Harnoncourt–Jean-Pierre
Ponnelle Monteverdi stagings, where the music is performed as
"authentically" as possible but the staging is just as far removed
from authenticity. And the role of the stage director is paramount:
it can embrace a "production concept," an individualized way of
looking at a specific opera, that might be a central part of what
composer and librettist intended, might refer to the opera only
tangentially in a single aspect, or might be what a director infers
is the "subtext" or inner spirit of the work, perhaps contradicted
by the surface. Or it might be a calculated effort to go quite consciously and deliberately *against* the opera.

This feature is just as revolutionary, for until recently authenticity has been the given: not the musical authenticity mentioned
above, but an attempt to reproduce as exactly as possible, in today's performing conditions, what the composer and librettist put
down. The nineteenth century no less than the eighteenth was a
playground for improvisation within the loose framework of the
opera: arias added, removed, and shuffled about; ballets on other
subjects by other composers interpolated between the acts or
played afterward or before. Wagner and Verdi, each in his own
way, sought to impose order on this license, to the point where, at
the end of the nineteenth and the beginning of the twentieth
century, new operas by Puccini could be presented only if the
opera house reproduced the exact sets, costumes, and direction
specified by Puccini through his agents, the house of Ricordi (artistic purity here being wedded to financial profit for both Ricordi
and Puccini). Conductors like Mahler and, more rigorously, Tos-

canini elevated this concept of fidelity to the composer to religious levels. There was but one Right Way, typified by Wanda Landowska's bit of nonsense: "You play Bach your way; I'll play him his way."

Much of this is now past history, at least visually, in opera production. The eyes have it, as McLuhan and others have remarked; and what the eyes see is ultimately more stimulating to a general audience than what the ears hear. In fact, what the ears hear everywhere except opera houses is now regularly reinforced by electronic amplification to become just as stimulating as the visual input.

Similarly, an imposed unity, whether philosophic (usually Marxist in orientation) or personal (the vision of a director) provides an easily apprehended, centralizing organization that draws together the necessarily disparate operatic elements into a single, cohesive entity. This simplification is on one level persuasive, and on another propagandistic; and if it reduces scope, it also provides punch.

There are a multitude of reasons why these revolutionary changes have invaded, taken hold, and become accepted parts of operatic production today. The fundamental one is that opera has become a more integral part of society's artistic yearnings than is suggested by its time-honored depiction as "an exotick entertainment" for the very few. The very few may include the scholars and pedants, but they are primarily the vocal buffs, who invariably care less about the setting or the point of view than about singers and singing. *La Gioconda* and *Andrea Chénier,* minor efforts by traditional artistic standards and especially minor ones when set against *Fidelio* or *Le nozze di Figaro* or *Die Meistersinger,* are cherished by the opera buff. If opera were a closed form appealing primarily to them, singing would remain paramount. But opera has always appealed to a larger audience, and that audience responds to the visual.

Another factor inextricably bound up with this revolution is the closed form of the repertory itself. Repertory opera is confined to a small group of works played again and again, and the lack of a continuing genesis of a significant number of repertory operas in the later twentieth century has made opera companies increasingly dependent on the earlier works. If there is an audience larger than the opera buffs, and if—as in the United States, Germany, England, and France—opera performances have grown in number and in importance to the society, a fiftieth *Traviata* will have less and less attraction if performed in the same sets and with the same production, albeit one "faithful to Verdi's ideas." We demand constant novelty, and we demand to be entertained.

I suspect another reason is the lack of individually exciting singers and/or conductors. Whether the Golden Age has departed or not, the proliferation of operatic performances and the availability of money to hire expensive singers has meant that the limited number of top-level singers (and even second-line singers) has been stretched thinner and thinner. And if the *Traviata* we are given has no special vocal distinction, how better to spice it up for an audience than to try something different in the one area that can be treated with novelty: the staging. On the highest artistic level, Walter Felsenstein's successes in opera with essentially minor singers are symbolic; but opera production today has shown that you don't need the genius of a Felsenstein to get into the newspapers.

The arguments as to the merits and demerits of this staging revolution are the hottest current debate in opera, and far more inflammatory than the Grand Game of vocal comparisons mentioned in the last chapter. Those in favor see the developments as indications of opera staying with the times as a "relevant" and fruitful art form, as well as one that appeals to a younger, wider audience. Those opposed see the developments as striking at the base of opera's being, of imposing willful, solipsistic, and often antimusical decisions upon a work, thus negating its musical core for the sake of extraneous considerations. Emotion rules, and its passion is more intense than those of the operatic characters.

The Metropolitan Opera, that bastion of conservatism, has stood aloof from most of this turmoil, to the relief of some and the cold disdain of others. Its experiments with the audacious have been few, and to the Jacobins timid; the most notable recent example was the borrowed (from San Francisco) production of Wagner's *Der fliegende Holländer* by Ponnelle in 1979, which aroused a storm akin to that onstage in the first act, and which was sent back whence it came with no regrets. The house of Caruso is not the venue for this sort of flagrant upstaging of the voices. The Met's experiments—seen most comprehensively, if in attenuated form, in the stagings of John Dexter—are modest: the triumphal scene in *Aida* played at night or, in Colin Graham's staging of *Traviata*, Father Germont's appearance at Flora's party in street clothes rather than evening dress (a touch that escapes 99 percent of the audience).

There is a solid reason beyond the usual conservative, singer-oriented nature of the Met that this restraint obtains. The Met, a house subsidized by its public and not by federal monies, must constantly watch expenses. A core repertory opera is expected to remain on view for a decade at least, and to see hard use during that time. Many casts will shuttle in and out, and these must be rehearsed in a minimum of time. But one of the posits of a new look at old operas is that this is a special staging, presented in an unusual way and depending on a break with traditional ideas of the opera and its characters. Thus, once the first cast and the director are gone, the next cast will fall into the old, timeworn habits.

Moreover, these stagings are often tied to the immediate; and as one of many possible interpretations, such a production is limited in scope. What may be provocative and even apposite in 1980 will become increasingly obvious and superficial, if not irrelevant, by 1985, once the novelty has worn off. Patrice Chéreau's staging of the *Ring* at Bayreuth, a sensation in 1976, has already been retired and has become part of operatic history.

The Met, therefore, does not incline to experimentation with repertory works, since each new production costs upward of four hundred thousand dollars. Better to be "authentically" safe than "experimentally" sorry.

These exigencies of repertory influenced Dexter's productions—the mannered gestures he called for in *Aida* disappeared during the first run—so that today, many of their individual touches have been subsumed by operatic business-as-usual. The *Rigoletto* was still saddled by the problems imposed by its unit set and displayed its original anachronistic touches, such as the melodramatic light show at the end of the opera, which transformed Rigoletto's grief at the loss of his daughter into farce. But the performance on October 19 was judged, by those in the house and those in the press, less for its director's quirks than for the qualities of the singers.

Perhaps that is the most galling riposte: that despite the smoke and fire of the controversy, the frantic efforts of the stage director are forgotten after the first few performances. And then it's back to Grand Game time, with Matteo Manuguerra being compared to Milnes (or Warren, or Bruson, or Cappuccilli) as Rigoletto, and Judith Blegen acclaimed for her floating pianissimo as Gilda.

The Met is presenting four new productions this year of four popular operas, and none of those productions departs radically from the norm. That may or may not be good artistic sense. But it certainly is good business sense—if not in the short run, then in the long run. If the new *La Bohème* will be performed twenty times this season, and goodness knows how many times over the next few years, it had better, in *Variety*'s lingo, have the legs.

O C T O B E R

26	27	28	29	30	31	31
Die Frau	**La traviata**	**Rigoletto**	**Die Frau**	**Il trittico**	**Rigoletto**	**Tosca**
ohne	*Rescigno;*	*Patanè;*	**ohne**	*Levine;*	*Patanè;*	*Patanè;*
Schatten	*Malfitano,*	*Blegen,*	**Schatten**	*Scotto,*	*Blegen,*	*Zylis-Gara,*
Leinsdorf;	*M. Cortez,*	*Jones,*	*Leinsdorf;*	*Berini,*	*Jones,*	*Giacomini,*
Marton,	*Bruson*	*Lloveras,*	*Marton,*	*Moldoveanu,*	*Lloveras,*	*Quilico*
Roberts,		*Manuguerra,*	*Nilsson,*	*Ciannella,*	*Manuguerra,*	
Cornell,		*Hines*	*Dunn,*	*MacNeil,*	*Hines*	
Brenneis,			*Brenneis,*	*Bacquier*		
Nentwig			*Nentwig*			

The Comprimarios

O n Saturday, October 31, Puccini's *Tosca* entered the repertory. It is another ever-popular work which is never long absent in any opera house. The protagonists—the volatile, amorous Tosca, her upright, liberty-loving Cavaradossi, and the suave, evil Baron Scarpia—have all been played by generations of stars. Here, they were undertaken by solid company artists; I will bypass their contributions in favor of those made by a singer who played the very small role of the Sacristan, Renato Capecchi.

Capecchi, born in Cairo in 1923, has had a distinguished career as a baritone. He first sang at the Met from 1951 to 1954 in such roles as Germont and Marcello in *La Bohème*.

The Sacristan may not have much to sing (he appears only in the first act), but in this opera fashioned from a very actor-conscious play, everyone makes a stage contribution—which is one reason why *Tosca* remains so popular. When the Sacristan enters, he has the stage to himself, and later he interjects comments during the first of the tenor's two arias, "Recondita armonia."

As can be imagined, this gives him a series of opportunities to gain the notice of the audience with stage business, and even to upstage the evening's tenor, as that old rascal Salvatore Baccaloni was reputed to have done on the Met's stage on various occasions.

Capecchi, however, confined himself to the traditional, while adding one personal touch. When he took holy water from the font below the Madonna's statue, he did a little obeisance by dipping his head while stretching one leg behind him. He received the accolade of a laugh. (Unfortunately, he made the mistake of repeating the exact gesture before his last exit—inappropriately, since he had just been excoriated for incompetence by Scarpia, and his reigning idea at that moment would not be to linger, but to escape from that threatening presence as soon as possible.) Yet the comic figure of the Sacristan gives texture and contrast to the first act, and thus the singer who has appeared in that role has contributed to whatever success the evening has.

Opera houses do not run only on the fuel generated by the stars. And any opera house that considers itself more than a collection of names for an evening of vocalism must develop and have available a group of lesser singers who form the ensemble, the day-to-day cohesiveness of the company. These singers, known in the trade as "comprimarios," have house contracts calling for a certain number of performing roles and a group of "cover," or under-studied, ones, and they are seen more often onstage than anyone but the chorus.

Occasionally, these singers are beginning in opera and on their way to much bigger roles; James McCracken is a prime example, graduating from the Messenger in *Aida* to Radames. But more likely, they are singers who have made the smaller roles their *Fach*—another trade word, which denotes the special area of competence of an artist. And from time to time there are singers who after respectable, even illustrous, careers decide to spend the twilight of their vocal days playing smaller roles.

This does not mean that the comprimarios are lost in opera's necessary busy-ness. Many smaller roles are extremely rewarding, can justifiably garner applause when the lead ones do not, and are integral to the opera in question. Any opera lover can make a list of such roles—the Idiot in *Boris Godunov,* Monsieur Triquet in *Eugene Onegin,* Benoît and Alcindoro in *La Bohème,* and the servants in *Les Contes d'Hoffmann*—and the success of their turns in the limelight contributes to the success of the opera performance.

This is not always immediately evident. I remember being told, during one of the periodic financial crises at the Met, that one Board member had in all seriousness put forward the idea that, in order to save money, all small roles be eliminated; the operas would be given as musical highlights with the top singers. After all, if in 1900 no one paid a nickel to see the conductor's back (as general manager Maurice Grau said), no one but family and friends paid to hear the Flora in *La traviata.*

Yet one of the surer tests of an opera company's quality remains the level of accomplishment of the comprimarios, for it is these artists in the lesser roles who give the company its depth of expertise, its very tone—even more than the artists in the orchestra pit or in the chorus. In minor opera companies these roles are usually badly handled, either by neophytes lacking in stage presence and voice or by singers too broken down for anything but a pathetic impression. But in a good opera company, these singers can form the ensemble basis over which the lead roles sing the melody.

The Met has had a long and illustrious history of comprimario artists. In the recent past, there have been such notables as George Cehanovsky, Thelma Votipka, and Alessio de Paolis, and currently the stalwart tenor Charles Anthony (born Charles Anthony Caruso!) carries on the tradition. He and Cehanovsky were given the Met's first Metropolitan Opera Company Service Awards in December for their contributions.

James Levine, when he became music director, arranged to bring back to the company respected older singers with decades of operatic experience to undertake some of these roles, among them Fedora Barbieri, Italo Tajo, and Renato Capecchi.

Later in 1981–82, this policy was brilliantly exemplified by bringing over from France the noted French tenor and, latterly, comprimario specialist Michel Sénéchal to sing the comic roles in Offenbach's *Les Contes d'Hoffmann*. His silent "duet" with the doll Olympia became one of the season's acting triumphs, regularly stopping the show. But what was more delightful to the opera buff was his handling of Frantz's couplets in the Antonia act. The song tells of the value of "method" in training for singing and dancing, and its comedy lies in the fact that Frantz, old and deaf, can do neither. Usually the turn is done for easy laughs. Yet, when Sénéchal sang the words "la méthode" in a cracked and quavery tenor, he proceeded to show that method vocally: he sang it in an old man's recollection of the vocal technique of fil di voce (thread of voice), and followed it with a minuscule messa di voce (a vocal technique of swelling and diminishing volume on a single tone, much favored by earlier singers but practically unheard today). This vocal display escaped most of the audience (and at least one working critic), but it constituted some of the most accomplished singing qua singing done in the house all year.

The Sciarrone—one of Scarpia's henchmen—of the October 31 *Tosca* was baritone Russell Christopher, who has been part of the comprimario corps at the Met since his debut in December 1963. He has thus sung in both the old and the new house, under three managements.

I asked him about his years as a comprimario.

"In the old house we were one big happy family," he said, "because Bob Herman's office was right down the hall from the stage door. [Herman was an assistant manager under Bing.] There was the feeling of one group of people putting on opera. Now, the place is too big: the offices are in an ivory tower far away, and I rarely see anyone in management. It's not a happy family atmosphere anymore; it's impersonal and distant."

When Christopher came to the Met, from singing small but promising roles at the San Francisco Opera such as Silvio in *Pagliacci*, he might have hoped for larger roles, but he soon was disabused. In 1964 Bing sent conductor George Schick to tell him that although he was a reliable artist and cover for smaller roles, he could expect nothing more than that.

"With Bing, you knew where you stood."

Christopher performed many comprimario roles through the latter Bing years, and under Schuyler Chapin he was allowed to graduate to larger ones, such as Alberich in *Siegfried.* When Chapin left, Christopher went back to comprimario status.

"Of course, I never really wanted to spend a career as a comprimario, the way colleagues like Andrea Velis have. I have always regretted not singing, for instance, Sharpless or Father Germont in the house, although I did sing fifteen Germonts in student matinees. But what is important is that you do your best. I believe that a comprimario should feel that whatever he sings, it's as if he were the lead; and even on nights when I'm singing the fifth or sixth performance of an opera, I never slough off—once I'm on-stage, I do my best. I rarely cancel, and I know my music—that's a big asset."

In the late 1960s, the Met instituted a "plan artist" arrangement under which forty-four singers were guaranteed a full year's employment in a variety of roles. Levine and Dexter cut this group to half, and there are some artists who are getting paid but do not get to sing. (Under current union contracts, the laying-off of a contract singer takes three years to effectuate, which is one reason why the full impact of a new management's policies cannot be felt until well into the life of that management.)

Christopher notes: "I love getting paid, but all of us want to work. I'm always happier with a lot to do. But this year, for instance, I'm doing a lot until January, and then I have nothing—not even a cover role—until I start rehearsals in the spring for the tour. I don't think there is an equitable distribution of roles over a season."

Christopher sees the influence of the spoken stage invading the Met.

"They're now casting for physical types, as they do on Broadway. In the old days, it was said you needed three things in order to sing at the Met: voice, voice, and voice. Now, I'm not so sure. Whether you look the part is more important, and they bring in artists for one or two operas who never become part of the company."

This trend of casting to physical type has also been noted by others as endemic to opera throughout the United States. Fat singers who are not named Pavarotti or Caballé are often passed over or relegated to comic roles, and they are encouraged to lose weight rather than to improve their voices.

Yet even more important is another attitude at the Met, which was summed up in the subhead of a Sunday *New York Times Magazine* article on Anthony Bliss: "The chief of New York's major opera company has restored it to solvency. But is it, as his critics charge, at the cost of artistic quality?" (September 20, 1981)

That question is the one most constantly posed, backstage and in opera circles. Rightly or wrongly, this perception influences morale. But some of Christopher's colleagues view the situation in a different light.

Soprano Betsy Norden has been a company soloist since 1972, and she began in the Met chorus in 1969. This season she sings several small roles. Norden is immensely grateful for the opportunities provided by a repertory house like the Met.

"I'm married, with two small children. I like to be home, and if I weren't at the Met, I would have to spend time traveling, or go abroad for a career. Renata Scotto combines a career with children, but it is at a cost. I have no desire to do it—I couldn't do it. But I don't have to. The Met is the greatest house, and here I have an opportunity for learning and for meeting people from here and abroad. I feel like a village fool because I can only speak two languages in this house!"

Norden's position as a house artist allows her to study with coaches in the house whenever she wants to for the roles she is singing and to arrange for any study for other roles she would like to add to her repertory.

"It's a compromise, of course. There are roles I'd like to do but probably never will in the house. My children are big enough now so that next year I have accepted an invitation to be in San Francisco for six weeks. But I know I can come back to the Met.

"It's phenomenal what I have learned since I've been here. I was tremendously confident when I came to the Met, but when I consider how much I didn't know then . . . !"

Norden feels that the current management—and Levine, because of his infectious enthusiasm—boosts morale in the house, and that this leads to better performances.

Thus, the question of morale can be seen from more than one angle. And in the final analysis, it is evidenced not by the reactions of this or that singer, but by the product as it comes across to the audience.

			N O V E M B E R			
2	3	4	5	6	7	7
La traviata	**Il trittico**	**Rigoletto**	**Die Zauberflöte**	**Tosca**	**Il trittico**	**Rigoletto**
Rescigno;	*Levine;*	*Patanè;*		*Patanè;*	*Levine;*	*Patanè;*
Malfitano,	*Scotto,*	*Blegen,*	*Foster;*	*Zylis-Gara,*	*Scotto,*	*Blegen,*
Raffanti,	*Berini,*	*Jones,*	*Donat,*	*Giacomini,*	*Taillon,*	*Jones,*
Bruson	*Moldoveanu,*	*Lloveras,*	*Battle,*	*Quilico*	*Moldoveanu,*	*Lloveras,*
	Ciannella,	*Manuguerra,*	*Kuebler,*		*Creech,*	*Manuguerra,*
	MacNeil,	*Hines*	*Allen,*		*MacNeil,*	*Hines*
	Bacquier		*Talvela*		*Bacquier*	

Translation

O n November 5 Mozart's *Die Zauberflöte* entered the repertory, in the acclaimed production designed by Marc Chagall. The program carried a line reading, "The Metropolitan Opera is grateful to the Rosenthal Studio-Linie for its generous gift toward the revival of this production"—a line that is carried, with only a change of name, on (the Met hopes) each revival of the year. But the funds, in whatever amount, must not have stretched very far in terms of refurbishing the decor: examining the gauzy drop curtains painted to look like everyone's idea of Chagall's colors, animals, and winsome humanoids, one could easily see shreds of dangling cloth, and burlap covering a gaping hole.

But the monster in the first scene made its invariable humorous impression as it cavorted and died; and thus the tone was set for this Papageno-eyed view of Mozart's last opera.

The opera was sung in German.

This is consistent with Met policy, which is to perform operas in their original language insofar as possible. (The current management, moreover, has taken the position that when it does translate an opera into English, it will present the revival in the original, as it did with Poulenc's *Les Dialogues des carmélites*.) Thus, the dialogue in *Die Zauberflöte*, which binds together the Singspiel's musical numbers, and which was given in fuller form than is usually the case in American opera houses, was spoken in German. To judge by the occasional ripples of laughter in the audience, the dialogue was comprehensible (both in audibility and in the understanding of the language) to a fair portion of the attendees.

The whole question of opera in the original or in the vernacular of the audience is another ongoing, and unresolvable, operatic debate. It is not so much a Grand Game as a cannonading from rival fortresses of entrenched opinion. The battle lines are so hardened, and the arguments so encrusted with certainty, that only limited compromise is possible. If the opera is in some out-of-the-way language (Czech, Finnish, at times Russian), it can justifiably be translated; or if the opera is a comedy, with spoken dialogue that needs to be understood, it can also be taken into the vernacular. In fact, the performances of *Zauberflöte* on the Met's 1982 spring tour will become *The Magic Flute*, in the Ruth and Thomas Martin translation.

There are practical reasons for doing opera in the original. In Germany, for instance, young singers learn the core repertory in standard German translations, which up to recently have been used for most performances. But young American singers learn their roles in the original and are loath to learn operas in a translation they may use only a few times. Thus, if forced, singers will opt for "standard English translations"—which have the patina of age and wide currency, but also that of mediocrity—in preference to newer, perhaps better, renditions of the text. The bigger the reputation of the singer, the less likely it is that he or she will be persuaded to learn a new text. In a house dependent, even with modified stagione practices, upon changes of cast within a production, any translation is a dangerously risky business. Better to perform it in the original, garner the plaudits of the purists, and strike one worry from the list.

The translation argument, in the end, is less one of immediacy than one of philosophy. If opera is meant to be more than vocalise and to be understood in terms of the specific words, then translation is a necessity, unless an audience is tri- or quatrolingual. But if opera is considered first and foremost singing, then general story, then visual delight, and finally the words (and quite often, to be sure, the words are the weakest aspect of the four), better to leave it in the original, and justify the decision by arguments about the absolute fit of the word settings, or how the language flows with the music in German or Italian or French in a way an English translation does not.

The posits are fundamentally unanswerable, for the arguments are but smokescreens for the underlying certainty of opinion. Just as it will do no good to point to the numerous examples of bad word-setting of major operatic composers, it will also do no good to point out the egregious gaffes in various translations.

But there are two other factors that enter into any discussion of whether opera should be performed in the original or translated into the vernacular, and these are less often mentioned. The primary one is clarity of diction.

Beverly Sills once rightly remarked, when asked about translation, that it was not so much a matter of whether an opera was done in English as whether the artists could sing it so that it was comprehensible. Many American singers are never taught to enunciate their native language, for many voice teachers feel that it is the musical line, or the notes themselves, rather than the music through the words, that counts. They thus push the words back into the throats of their singers so that they emerge coated and obscured by the music. Joan Sutherland is the classic example of the "Music First" school; even when she is singing in her native tongue, she is largely unintelligible.

The "French" school of singing, which puts diction first, has long been in disfavor, even in France, although it only took to a greater extreme what was being taught in Italy. To listen to the Italian diction of the French baritone Gabriel Bacquier or the Italian bass Italo Tajo in the Met's current production of Puccini's *Il* *trittico* is to appreciate what is meant by singing enunciation. No matter that Bacquier is well over fifty and Tajo well over sixty: there is a strength and propulsiveness to the music when it is combined actively with the words that carries both into the auditorium and into the listeners' ears.*

Which brings us to the other factor. As has already been suggested, we today listen with our eyes when in the theater, and tend to turn up the volume controls when listening at home. Pop music, of course, does this for us, as do Broadway musicals. Our ears have become extremely lazy, and we have given up trying to understand barely intelligible words.

We have, in addition, come a long way from the audience of Haydn's day, which was largely made up of performer-aristocrats. Today's audience is by and large an amateur one, at best passionately interested in music, but unable to analyze it with any degree of knowledge—and not really interested in doing so. And this audience is frankly more interested in the totality of the operatic experience, and in the voices, than in the specifics of word setting.

Thus, the arguments on both sides will never resolve into agreement, and managements will continue to approach the idea of translation on an ad hoc basis. Those who want the words but do not know the language must buy the libretto, which is sold throughout the house at every performance. Or if they watch on television, they can take advantage of a singularly effective compromise and read the English subtitles while the opera is going on.

This last may be the best solution. In the opera house, however,

---

*David Hamilton, in *Keynote*, April 1982, p. 22, makes an interesting and hitherto unmentioned point. The old school of opera singers learned opera first in their native languages. Because of this, their recordings of opera arias in their native languages often had an immediacy of communication and a knowledge of vocal articulation lacking when they recorded the same excerpts in the original. Since today's American singers tend to learn everything "in the original," they project a kind of all-purpose, neutral singing style, suited to every language but never really responsive to the words or the characterization, for those languages are neither natural to the singers nor ingrained in them through years of exposure. In the bargain, too many American singers have never been taught how to sing their own language.

the normal response will continue to be to try and figure out what is going on by the general flow of the action, and bone up on the synopsis during the intermission. The very unintelligibility of so much that ideally should be understandable may cause anguish to the cognoscenti, but it does not seem to bother the casual opera-goer, who accepts that as part of the "opera experience"; and it certainly does not ruffle the opera buff, who came anyway for the voices, not the text. The stretches of spoken German in *Die Zauberflöte* must be endured by the those who do not understand the language. The crucial dialogue between Tamino and the Speaker in front of the Temple in Act I may go over most heads, but that is included in the price of admission. If you can't understand it even in English, you might as well not understand it in the original.

N O V E M B E R						
9	10	11	12	13	14	14
Tosca	**Die**	**Il trittico**	**Rigoletto**	**Die**	**Tosca**	**Il trittico**
Patanè;	**Zauberflöte**	*Levine;*	*Patanè;*	**Zauberflöte**	*Patanè;*	*Levine;*
Zylis-Gara,	*Foster;*	*Scotto,*	*Devia,*	*Foster;*	*Zylis-Gara,*	*Scotto,*
Giacomini,	*Donat,*	*Taillon,*	*Jones,*	*Donat,*	*Giacomini,*	*Taillon,*
Quilico	*Battle,*	*Moldoveanu,*	*Alexander,*	*Battle,*	*Milnes*	*Moldoveanu,*
	Kuebler,	*Creech,*	*Manuguerra/*	*Kuebler,*		*Creech,*
	Allen,	*MacNeil,*	*Glossop,*	*Allen,*		*MacNeil,*
	Talvela	*Bacquier*	*Hines*	*Talvela*		*Bacquier*

Television

L ight levels have been adjusted . . ." read the note in the program for Puccini's *Il trittico* on October 11 and 14. The light levels onstage had been changed because the operas were being televised; and television, even with today's sophisticated equipment, requires a higher light level than that often employed in the opera house. The stage needs to be kept constantly bright, even when an opera calls for darkness.

The management willingly submits to this often grievous alteration of its artistic product because it respects, and indeed defers to, the power of television.

It has been suggested that the major area of development in finding new audiences for opera in recent years has been the "theatricalizing" of the form—that is, making the performance an immediately involving experience through some sort of updating to today's concerns and shifting the emphasis from the singer, who may or may not act, to the singing actor. But others feel that, important (if abused) as this development is, the major area of development for opera is in television.

There is no doubt that putting the Metropolitan Opera on television has added more than a new dimension to its renown. Since 1931, the Met has been broadcasting performances (in fact, there was a broadcast from the stage in 1910!), mostly on Saturday afternoons, to radio audiences in the United States and Canada, but the audience for these broadcasts has remained largely stable over the past two decades. Since the Met quite consciously sets itself forward as the national opera house as well as a basic American cultural resource, it must—in order to attract government no less than private monies—appeal to more than just the New York–area audience. It does this in part through the radio and in part through the annual spring tour.

The spring tour has always been a source of unease to many in the house, and that unease is growing. In many of the tour cities, the Met's visit is less an artistic than a social occasion, and the best tickets are reserved for the inner circle of those who can afford the very steep prices. All management efforts notwithstanding, the tour performances are rarely on the level of those in the Lincoln Center house and are too often more dependent upon star singers (who are increasingly reluctant to tour) than on the opera. In certain cities, such as (most notoriously) Cleveland, the size of the auditorium in which the Met performs may accommodate anyone wishing to buy tickets, but at an unaffordable artistic price. The auditorium there is a convention hall, which saw the nomination of two presidential candidates and is used for circuses. Its seating is "reduced" to eighty-eight hundred for the Met, it has no orchestra pit, and its miked acoustics give a sound that one observer called "similar to a 1930s opera recording." It is increasingly evident to those in the audience that what they see and hear onstage on tour is not only unrepresentative of the Met, but entirely different from the same productions they see on "Live from the Met" telecasts, so that the excuses of the management (What are we going to do for two months, with our year-long union contracts?) and the provision for a round of partying and society events, and the opportunity to show off new gowns and hairdos, is being bought at a price that devalues the Met itself.

The move into television has meant that the Met has opened itself to a far larger prospective audience. The results have been dramatic enough to demonstrate that while radio continues to be important on a week-to-week, continuing basis, television exposure is exponentially more valuable.

Every American opera company of any stature would dearly love to tap this market, and several have, but none more often than the Met. In 1981–82, the Met presented four "Live from the Met" performances.

The term "Live from the Met," which the Met uses to distinguish its series from another PBS series, "Live from Lincoln Center," is only partly accurate. What is meant is that the telecast opera is a live subscription performance in the opera house, not a special television staging or one made in an empty house or before an invited or lower-price-scaled audience. Of the four operas presented, one (*La traviata*) was recorded the previous spring during a live telecast to Europe and presented to American audiences in the fall of 1981; the Met's current cast and conductor are different. One (*Rigoletto*) was given on a day-delay basis; *La Bohème* was telecast live to Europe and shown in the United States four days later. The fourth, *Il trittico*, shown in the eighth week on Saturday night, November 14, was "live" in that the event was transmitted as it occurred, which resulted in one gaffe: a thirty-second interruption of signal caused by a malfunctioning relay switch (the repeat telecast was complete).

A delicate balancing act goes into the choice of the operas. Texaco, the longtime Met sponsor, absents itself from the selection process, but is obviously eager that there be a mix of the popular along with the fringe repertory. James Levine is equally eager to present operas like *Lulu* or *Mahagonny*, which do especially poorly in terms of audience. The superstars all want television exposure (rumor had it that *Rigoletto* was in the 1981–82 repertory only because Pavarotti wanted to do it on television), and of course superstars guarantee a bigger audience. But no singer is supposed to dominate the Met, and so appearances on radio and television, on opening nights, and in new productions must be carefully balanced and distributed among the roster of stars. Also, an opera should be technically right for television. Wagner operas are avoided because of their length and often because of their scenic problems. *Rigoletto,* on the other hand, may be an eyesore onstage in the Met's current production, but it works quite well when televised. The Met is aware that the operas thus enshrined on tape are historical documents for future viewing, and naturally wishes to avoid the inevitable subroutine disasters that occur in every season. Finally, the televised operas should be given over the length of the season and not bunched, for even if an opera is not telecast "live," the Met likes the telecasts to come close to the actual performance date.

Home television is still a picture from a small box: the qualities that emerge most strongly are not necessarily those that impress themselves on an audience in the opera house. The sound is still primitive, unless one listens to the simultaneous radio broadcasts in stereo; and even those, no matter how fine the equipment, present different sound than that heard at the Met. In the case of the star of the *Trittico* evening, Renata Scotto (who as a tour de force appeared in all three operas, though Puccini never wanted this), the radio/television sound had the merit of diffusing her shrill high notes, which registered less acidly than they did in the house.

Television is a medium congenial to the close-up, the facial expression, and a severe gestural restraint; it is less adept at suggesting depth, size, or spectacle. Unfortunately, the former are de-emphasized in opera, while the latter qualities are often highlighted on the Met's huge stage. Trying to project for an audience of almost four thousand, an opera singer, usually unconsciously, enlarges his conception. If he is not an actor, he will portray the classic operatic wooden Indian. Either way, the result is alien to television and serves to segregate opera performance into its own discrete category. Similarly, television may favor a singer who does not communicate well from stage to auditorium, and it also favors smaller, more focused voices over louder, less pointed ones.

Thus, the whole problem of televising opera, and of televising live performances, is alive with questions. Is the television viewer seeing and hearing what the in-house ticket buyer is? Is the televised performance changed from the nontelevised one in ways that make it more acceptable to the camera eye, but work against the enjoyment of those who have paid full price to see and hear the opera in the house? What effect has the camera (there are in fact five cameras) on the singers? Do they play to it, as Pavarotti did in an exaggerated way, at the expense of his leading lady, in the televised *L'elisir d'amore* of spring 1981? Or do they tone down their conceptions, as some people felt Beverly Sills did when her Norina in *Don Pasquale* was televised? Are good singers who happen to be poor actors avoided, and are singers who look the part being chosen in preference to those who sound right?

Renata Scotto is a very good example of an opera singer who delivers both on television and in the opera house, especially in the verismo operas that are her specialty. She was in the first telecast (*La Bohème*) of the current "Live from the Met" series.* Her conceptions are always very carefully calculated, yet in Puccini the mannered quality of her gestures and, at times, of her singing is usually overcome by the passion of the writing. Seeing and hearing her in the house on Wednesday and on television three nights later, I was aware of certain shifts of emphasis—not, I think, occasioned by changes in her conception so much as her being responsive to the differing demands of stage and television performance.

The latent sexuality of Scotto's portrayal of the barge master's wife, Giorgetta, in the first opera, *Il tabarro*, was as vivid on television as it was in the house, although the cross-cutting of images that television demands meant that the unity of her portrayal was

---

*The first in-house telecast was the opening-night *Otello* in 1948, but the first Met telecast (a studio performance of opera excerpts) took place on March 10, 1940, and was sent out to "two thousand TV fans."

not documented. Yet her Suor Angelica, in the second opera, came across better in the house than on television.

This is perhaps the fault of the opera, which is an exercise in the transfigured sentimental, a genre well out of current fashion—particularly on television, which has its own categories of fantasy—and extant only in the opera house. Angelica has borne a child out of wedlock and has been banished by her aunt to a convent. The tormented woman lives only for news of her child; and when she is brutally informed that he is dead, she takes poison. At the last moment Angelica awakes to the realization of her mortal sin of suicide, but she is saved by the intervention of the Virgin Mary, who brings her the child; she dies forgiven. In the Met production, neither the Virgin nor the child appears: the moment is suggested by the magical effect of stage lighting. Angelica receives the babe in pantomime.

At the Met, the combination of the ecstatic music, the staging, and Scotto's acting of the final scene was extremely effective. On television, however, the effect of the lighting was minimized and thus mostly lost, while the music did not overwhelm the senses as it did in the theater. The cameras were trained on Scotto in close-up and concentrated on her pantomime, which thus came across more as mannerism than as felt experience. And so the moment that is the culmination of the opera had the aura of contrivance rather than conviction.

It is lighting, as much as any single element, that defines the difference between the actuality of the performance and the "Live from the Met" telecast. A few years ago, the televised *Don Giovanni*—an opera that demands darkness for its most important scenes—was played in a blaze of noon, and *Elektra* (with Birgit Nilsson) was similarly brightened to the point of ridiculousness.

The *Elektra* is a good example, for Rudolf Heinrich had created the single set with the certainty that it would be dimly lit, as if by torchlight; and because of the low light levels he was able to project images onto the "sky" that enclosed the set. By adjusting the light levels for television, the ugliness and the sparsity of the set were cruelly revealed; it looked amateurish. And the projections simply could not be seen.

This situation had unintentional ramifications. One might have felt that the person who spent a good deal of money to see the opera in the house, performed and produced in a unified way, would feel cheated by the modifications imposed by television. But audiences have traditionally hated the low lighting levels favored by some of today's opera directors, and so the audience's reaction was strongly in favor of the brighter lighting—even if it made nonsense of the production and vitiated the sense of impending horror *Elektra* should create. After all, they came to see and hear Nilsson. Similarly, the singers onstage welcomed more light, for Heinrich had created a bumpy and treacherous stage floor which necessitated great care to avoid broken legs. (Audiences also do not seem to mind the cameras positioned to either side of the stage and in the aisles, just in front of the orchestra pit. I spoke to several subscribers who felt that attending a televised performance added to, rather than detracted from, the event.)

The Met's ex-director of productions, John Dexter, is outspoken in his opposition to in-house telecasts of regular performances. He feels that television is its own medium of communication, and that televised opera should be tailor-made, not dependent on a staged performance. Yet, given today's economics, there is little possibility of change in this area, at least as far as the Met is concerned.

"A 'Live from the Met' telecast costs us around four hundred thousand dollars," said Michael Bronson, director of the Met's media department and executive producer of the series. "A studio production would cost appreciably more; and if you want to film an opera on location, you're talking about, today, upwards of three million dollars."

Bronson prefers the performance telecasts to studio or location ones, with a few exceptions (e.g., Jean-Pierre Ponnelle's *Madama Butterfly*, which has attained the status of a classic opera film); he feels that the actual performance can provide an intensity and an energy lost if the voices are added later. "In our opening-night telecast of *Otello* [1979], the second-act duet with Domingo and Milnes was thrilling—and that gut excitement can't be duplicated."

When the Met first attempted television performances on a regular basis (the earlier telecasts were in every way experimental), the philosophy was to bring in the cameras and let them record what took place, without any interference. That philosophy has changed completely.

"We started work on the *Trittico* telecast last spring, when television director Kirk Browning and our stage director Fabrizio Melano began discussions. Browning's job is to tell the story in television terms. The same thing goes for the sound: you can't just put in a microphone and leave it there."

For *Il trittico*, cameras and microphones were positioned for the first opera, *Il tabarro*, which has a dual-level set and an awkward, fully constructed river barge downstage. After that opera, both cameras and microphones had to be repositioned for the other, more simply set, one-acters.

"We are, of course, dependent on costs, but within our budget we try to do things differently for television. For instance, the color white looks bad on television, so we dyed down Buoso's sheets and nightgown to off-white for the telecast."

Bronson admits the problems with lighting, but maintains that most of them arise because the Met has little time or money to reset the lighting board as efficiently as the lighting director, Gil Wechsler, would wish.

Televising performances is not as straitjacketing a task as one may think. During this season, the Met will televise a production it has already shown on "Live from the Met"—*Rigoletto*—albeit with a different cast. But this production will be visually different as well, for the director this time is Brian Large, and he sees the opera in another way than his colleague Kirk Browning, who directed it the first time.

Yet, in the final analysis, it is the impact around the country that justifies the expenditure for these telecasts. There has been little attempt so far to find out who watches—what age range, whether or not the viewers are operatically sophisticated, and so on. Viewers are asked to write in for free "teleguides" extracted from issues of *Opera News* (all names going into the Met's master file), and the response varies widely from opera to opera (Verdi's *Luisa Miller* brought in a large response, probably because of the work's unfamiliarity).

Bronson is unsure whether the telecasts have helped sell tickets to the operas shown or hindered these sales. The test with the unfamiliar operas, in any case, comes less in New York than in the tour cities, and the results are inconclusive. Certainly some viewers have been led to buy tickets for a one-time look at the opera house; but whether that one time leads to a mini-series subscription, or to a regular subscription, is another question.

Television exposure means national advertising of the product, on a scale much greater than the weekly radio broadcast. And even if the numbers are minuscule compared with network television (a New York–area Nielsen rating of 4 for *L'elisir d'amore* with Pavarotti was considered very good; *Lulu* garnered 0.9), it is an audience both "upscale" and loyal. (Public television stations like it when a Met telecast coincides with their pledge weeks; the hours of the telecast usually bring in large amounts of money for the station.)

Whether the future lies with public television, which is becoming ever more audience conscious, or with some sort of cultural ghetto cable is again uncertain, as is the marketing of past and future presentations as videodiscs or videotapes. The Met, always business minded, is exploring every avenue.

N	O	V	E	M	B	E	R

16	17	18	19	20	21	21
Rigoletto	**Tosca**	**Die**	**Il trittico**	**Rigoletto**	**Die**	**Tosca**
Patanè;	*Patanè;*	**Zauberflöte**	*Levine;*	*Patanè;*	**Zauberflöte**	*Patanè;*
Devia,	*Neblett,*	*Foster;*	*Scotto,*	*Devia,*	*Foster;*	*Neblett,*
Jones,	*Giacomini,*	*Donat,*	*Taillon,*	*Jones,*	*Donat,*	*Carreras,*
Alexander,	*Glossop*	*Battle,*	*Moldoveanu,*	*Alexander,*	*Battle,*	*Milnes*
Quilico,		*Kuebler,*	*Creech,*	*Manuguerra,*	*Kuebler,*	
Berberian		*Allen,*	*MacNeil,*	*Hines*	*Allen,*	
		Talvela	*Bacquier*		*Talvela*	

The Guild: Resource
or Cash Register?

During the ninth week, the house presented repetitions of four operas; but the real activity went on backstage, where preparations were going ahead for the first two new productions, the Stravinsky triple bill and *La Bohème*. Ticket sales were holding up quite well, and the excitement attendant on new productions was building.

That excitement extended to the offices of the Metropolitan Opera Guild, down Broadway from Lincoln Center, because the premiere of *La Bohème* would be a Guild benefit, and every effort was being made to sell all the tickets at benefit prices.

During any season, the Met, like all opera houses, gives the maximum share of its attention to its new productions. The work entailed by these productions always gives the house a beneficial infusion of spirit and morale—at least until the reviews appear. New productions are not always the best-remembered nights of a season, and some quietly sink without a trace (e.g., the Met's 1963 production of Massenet's *Manon*, not seen since 1965). But as something new, they are fundamental for a repertory house. A thirty-week season with fewer than three new productions is a sparse one; this year's five came about because one of them—*Così fan tutte*—had been deferred from last year.

New productions, however, are horrendously expensive, particularly for the Met, and that expense constantly grows. For many decades the costs have been beyond the ability of the company to fund entirely out of its regular budget, and the Met has had to turn to individual and (to a minimal extent) corporate contributors to come up with the monies. But as costs have risen, even this group has had to be backstopped by a Fund for Productions, created by the Met as a funding source when an individual production does not attract a single donor or group of donors.

The Fund for Productions and its allied money-raising groups— the Golden Horseshoe, the Patrons Program, the National Council, the Centennial Fund—are all antedated by the Metropolitan Opera Guild, founded in 1936. Earlier in its history, the Guild gave money for several new productions—notably the Lee Simonson *Ring* cycle of 1948.

The Guild, the almost single-handed creation of the dynamic Mrs. August Belmont, helped shore up the finances of the house in the later 1930s and was vital in channeling the enthusiasms of less affluent operagoers. As important as the job of saving the house from darkness was, however, it was not the only thing on Mrs. Belmont's mind. Education and the transmitting of enthusiasm about opera was equally important, and to that end the Guild did not stop at money raising, but created educational programs and began publishing *Opera News,* under the editorship of Mrs. John DeWitt Peltz, who later became the Met's first archivist.*

---

*Mrs. Peltz, a familiar, diminutive figure in the opera house and around the country at local Guild meetings, died in her sleep on October 23, 1981, after coming home from a performance of *Die Frau ohne Schatten.* I remember her for one charming, if not entirely accurate, statement: "Press agents are paid a lot to tell lies; critics are paid poorly to tell the truth."

The Guild today—under the leadership of Board President Katharine T. O'Neil—is a larger and more diverse organization than it was even fifteen years ago. Its membership, including National Members, who receive *Opera News* and the Guild's mailings, but have no ticket privileges, is around a hundred thousand; of these, the higher categories of members number over sixteen thousand. For these latter members, the Guild provides a ticket service, a series of free lectures, the opportunity to attend dress rehearsals, and the use of the Belmont Room, a Grand Tier–level lounge in the opera house. It also sponsors benefit premieres of new productions—this year, *La Bohème* and *Les Contes d'Hoffmann*—and gives an annual luncheon in the Grand Ballroom of the Waldorf-Astoria. In the last few years, it has donated about a million and a half dollars a year in direct contributions to the Association.

The relationship of the Guild to its parent body has never been entirely smooth. It is the only Met support organization separately incorporated, which has meant that, although its purpose has been to provide monies for the Met, it can control and has controlled its own programs outside the Met's direct surveillance, even though it has always had a partly overlapping board of directors. (In fact, the Guild has long been used as a tryout venue for future MOA board members, who graduate to the big league after commendable service.) The fierce independence that characterized Mrs. Belmont, however, has been reflected in her cherished creation on more than one occasion.

That independence is once again—and this time, perhaps, finally—being challenged by the Met management, which wishes to amalgamate the Guild into the parent organization for efficiency and cost savings. A protocol between the two has been negotiated by which the Guild will move its offices into the opera house and will transfer certain of its departments to the Association. Although the Guild will retain its identity and various privileges (e.g., choosing special events and running them through its own committees), the erosion of its independence is well advanced.

One of the areas of friction between the management and the Guild has always been *Opera News*. The Guild's magazine was created to be the voice of opera and of the Met to the public, and from early days was linked to the Saturday-afternoon broadcasts. It is often called the Met's house organ, and to an extent it is. But in the past two decades, under editors Frank Merkling and (currently) Robert Jacobson, it has become a year-round publication taking as its province all of opera, with emphasis on opera in the United States, and specifically at the Met. It regularly devotes issues to other major American opera companies and to notable productions of opera around the country.

For many years *Opera News* carried reviews of performances in the United States, Canada, and abroad, but never any reviews of the Met. This omission was rectified several years ago; but the editors must walk a tightrope in expressing their opinions of the Met, and some outsiders feel that the result is overshadowed by the implied restraints. Yet, to many opera lovers outside New York, the reviews of the Met in *Opera News* are their best contact with what is going on in the house.

Opera News must walk another tightrope: between those who want it to be a glossy magazine of pictures, chitchat, and flackery and those who want it to be a serious journal discussing, in reasonable depth, operas and Opera.

Specific examples of differences between the Met and the Guild are not, finally, important—the management has its difficulties with its own organizations, such as the National Council. What is important is the way the Met has over the years considered the role of the Guild. And that is, as a bottom line, the bottom line: i.e., as a money machine.

The Met expects the Guild to fulfill its monetary quota each year, and to that end the Guild has rigorously professionalized its entire operation. The complaint heard backstage that the Met has become a business ("Bliss only wants to sell T-shirts") has also been heard in the corridors of the Guild offices, now located in the American Bible Society Building at Broadway and Sixty-second Street. Gone are the volunteer ladies recruited by Mrs. Belmont to help save the Met; gone are the genteel lecture-teas at the Colony Club, with their aura of a time gone by; gone is the one-to-one relationship with the Guild's own ticket lady (all ticket orders are now filled at the Met, from information supplied by a computer); gone is the camaraderie engendered by the Guild's own box of fifty-five seats in the old house; and gone is the often raffish "annual event" in the opera house—free to Guild members—which provided fun and diversion to the evenings at the opera.

What has replaced this is a resolute pursuit of the opera dollar. *Opera News,* for instance, was begun as a forum for writing about opera and singers and as an educational tool; it was never regarded as a source of profit. As long as its costs did not jeopardize the Guild through excessive financial drain, *Opera News* was felt to be (by most Guild board members, at least) a vital asset: a voice for the Met and for opera to the public, and therefore an integral part of opera's outreach. But over the years, the pressure on *Opera News* to show not only a profit but, in current terminology, a "maximization of profit" has steadily increased. Geoff Peterson, the Guild's current managing director, is forthright about the magazine's role: "*Opera News*'s economic justification comes first and foremost, and then, of course, its educational mission."

If *Opera News* is the publication arm of the Guild, cannot its staff be put to use for other, related, publication purposes whose justification is economic? Thus, the Guild publishes the annual Met program book, including all the year's operas and artists, and sells it by mail, in the opera house, and on tour. It also publishes an engagement calendar, the teleguides, and one-shots for other Lincoln Center constituents, such as the New York Philharmonic. And, finally, it has begun *Ballet News,* to take advantage of the burgeoning interest in ballet nationwide, as well as add names to the Guild's mailing list.

The education department of the Guild has recently dropped the longtime run of student matinees in the opera house, in part because of scheduling problems, but mostly because of the costs, which were found impossible to underwrite. "The same money is more productive if it is applied elsewhere," says Peterson, who feels that the current programs, focused on preliminary music-theater appreciation in the schools, is a better way to introduce youngsters to opera. The Guild is working toward a national distribution of educational materials and audio-visual aids, and provides in-service courses and lectures for teachers as well as for the public. The aim is to market opera appreciation as professionally as possible, and through that marketing to sell opera as a vital cultural resource, to keep the name of the Met before the public— and, not incidentally, to show a profit, which the education department did (barely) in 1980–81.

Marketing, however, means merchandising, and the Guild has been caught up in the current crusade for the dollar popularized, if not invented, by its patron saint, Thomas Hoving, when he was at the other Met, the museum. The Guild's merchandising department was created in 1976; for 1981–82 the Guild projects a gross of almost two million dollars worth of sales, and a net of $158,000. The major share of this revenue comes from mail-order catalogues, with the Christmas catalogue providing almost a million dollars and the early fall catalogue half a million.

The catalogues list a wide variety of wares, from the strictly practical-educational librettos and scores, through recordings of Met singers, to all sorts of gift possibilities: mugs, ties, necklaces, ticket folders, scarves, towels—most with either a Met or an opera identification. Posters and prints are prized by the Guild, because the relative profit margin is much higher for them, and in addition they can appreciate in value in today's art market. (The "blue" Chagall poster made for the opening of the Lincoln Center house is now sold out, and is worth well over a thousand dollars.) The two "three-sheet" posters by David Hockney sell for $250 apiece.

The catalogue mailings are sent to the Met master file list. But, increasingly, they are also being sent to other, outside, lists: responses go onto the master file.

"This year for the first time we have sent these names an appeal for donations to the Met," said Peterson.

Peterson and his merchandising director, Paul Gruber, see plenty of opportunities for expansion of product lines that can be, in Gruber's words, "opera-ized" for future catalogues. They stress that, important as the money received is, another important factor is the communication afforded by the catalogues to people around the United States. This argument is accepted, albeit a whit more skeptically, by Thomas Russell, the Guild board member who is also chairman of the merchandising committee. He understands the value of the program, but questions the profitability.

"The profit figure does not take into account inventory costs," he said. The inventory itself is kept at the Met's huge new warehouse in Weehawken, New Jersey, and is therefore free of storage costs.

Merchandising, however, is likely here to stay. Even state-subsidized houses, such as London's Royal Opera at Covent Garden, have gone into the business, and it is only a matter of time before it spreads to the Continent.

The centennial anniversary is certain to be a bonanza for such endeavors. Already the Met has sent out a flyer offering "an extraordinary work of art in fine, hand-painted porcelain" representing (fittingly!) Enrico Caruso as Canio in *Pagliacci*. The edition is of five thousand, and each one costs five hundred dollars. Should it sell out, the gross receipts would be $2.5 million. And the Caruso is but the first of a series.

Similarly, the Met has joined with Time/Life Records to market a series of opera excerpts on disc, keyed to Met stars and including Met-oriented booklets.

As Christmas approaches, the "Met by Mail" offices at the Opera Guild are extremely active. There is a small line at the bottom of the order forms: "Suggested voluntary contribution (tax deductible): five dollars." Already by fall 1981, that suggestion had resulted in twenty-two thousand dollars in contributions.

		N O V	E M	B E R		
23	*24*	*25*	*26*	*27*	*28*	*28*
Il trittico	**Die**	**Rigoletto**	**Tosca**	**Die**	**Il trittico**	**Rigoletto**
Levine;	**Zauberflöte**	*Patanè;*	*Patanè;*	**Zauberflöte**	*Levine;*	*Patanè;*
Savova,	*Foster;*	*Devia,*	*Neblett,*	*Foster;*	*Savova,*	*Devia,*
Cruz-Romo,	*Donat,*	*Jones,*	*Carreras,*	*Donat,*	*Cruz-Romo,*	*Jones,*
Malfitano,	*Robinson,*	*Montane,*	*Milnes*	*Robinson,*	*Malfitano,*	*Alexander,*
Berini,	*Kuebler,*	*Manuguerra,*		*Kuebler,*	*Berini,*	*Manuguerra,*
Moldoveanu,	*Dickson,*	*Berberian*		*Allen,*	*Moldoveanu,*	*Hines*
Ciannella,	*Talvela*			*Talvela*	*Ciannella,*	
MacNeil,					*MacNeil,*	
Bacquier					*Bacquier*	

Backstage

T he backstage tour is another Metropolitan Opera Guild activity. Each year hundreds of such tours take place, because of their popularity with visitors, opera lovers, and touring groups. The huge backstage areas of the new Metropolitan Opera House provide a varied field of exploration of the differing crafts that go to make up an opera company. It is on these tours that one can get an inkling of the scale of Met operations, for if the sheer size and panoply of a gaudy Met production does make its effect in the auditorium, it is only when the pieces are taken apart backstage that the complexity of the production can be grasped.

Originally, the Met envisioned backstage facilities as the place where the production of an opera, which in the old house largely had to be farmed out, could be done under its supervision. Scenery could be built and painted, costumes could be constructed, and a basement would be large enough to store operas not being played.

Since the opening of the house, however, the Met has continued to be haunted by what was the major miscalculation in its construction. At one point, it was determined that there was not enough money to build the house plus its original office tower, which would have included space for the various management functions of the company and its ancillary groups. It was then determined to eliminate the tower and to shoehorn the offices into areas once meant for foyers and open spaces around the auditorium. (This resulted in the creation of two enormous blank walls facing the plaza, and someone had the inspired, but hardly artistically satisfactory, idea of commissioning Marc Chagall to cover them with murals.)

The decision to sacrifice office space for a completed and paid-for opera house, while in the long range wrong, was understandable, given the pressure to get Lincoln Center into full operation. What is less understandable was the second decision not to spend a smaller sum in order to put structure into place so that a tower could be built at some future date.

These decisions have meant that the Met has been constantly cramped for office space. But in 1981 the Met bought a warehouse across the Hudson River in Weehawken, New Jersey, which will consolidate its storage of sets and allow all set building to be done outside the house. (All but the largest sets can be transported through the Lincoln Tunnel.) Since this relocation will leave much empty room backstage, that space can now be used for offices for both the company and its support organizations.

In the future, there will still be some construction done in the house, and a number of costumes will continue to be stored there. But there is no question that a measure of the variety given by a backstage tour will be lost.

The tour I joined was one given a group of fifth- and sixth-grade students from New York's Trinity School who were taking an elective course in "opera appreciation." It was led by Mrs. Charles Gimber, a veteran of many tours, and who knows the opera house as intimately as the proverbial Phantom.

The Met backstage teems with people—stagehands setting up

or striking scenery or unrolling drops in painting areas upstairs, painters, costumers, carpenters, lighting and prop personnel, management, singers, members of the children's chorus, and numberless others. It is always a hive of activity. On this day, the light blue of David Hockney's designs for Stravinsky's fairy-tale *Le Rossignol* seemed in every corner, interspersed with the heavy-looking but light-weighing styrofoam Parisian roofs of *La Bohème*. Franco Zeffirelli, *Bohème*'s director, wandered by, closely followed by an assistant with a sheaf of papers. In his small office lined with color photographs of opera stars in costume, the Met's official photographer, James Heffernan, held court, while Martti Talvela as Boris Godunov glowered down from the wall. In the basement, the Tower of Babel battlement—the centerpiece of the *Rigoletto* set—loomed against the three-story wall.

"You can't fail to be impressed when you see all of this," said Mrs. Gimber, and the children, city-wise and inured to entertainment though they were, agreed. Tours, one going north and one going south, snaked past the gauze-covered figure of *Rossignol*'s mechanical nightingale (which would be operated from inside by a boy with earphones, cued by a stage manager to move the bird's head, click its bill, and flap its wooden wings).

Quiet reigned in the C-level orchestra rehearsal room, for this was late afternoon, and the orchestra had finished its tasks until evening. The room was bare except for piled-up chairs and a set of timpani. Quiet also reigned in the dressing-room area, ready with the names of the night's artists on each door—men to the right, ladies to the left—and the costumes lined up in the closet.

After an hour and a half, the children were sated with the sights of the stage, the three floors up and the three floors down.

"I don't know how many tours I've taken—it must be hundreds," said Mrs. Gimber. "But I always see something new every time. It's the best way I know to show people how complicated the Met operation is—how many, many parts there are to a performance. We'll miss some of it when they move to New Jersey, but there will still be plenty to see."

Considering that the Met payroll numbers over two thousand,

the house will never be empty. The constant work of building new sets, for the New York season and for the tour (which uses its own sets), refurbishing old ones, and starting on those for next year will go on, both in the house and across the Hudson.

"If you go backstage, you see why the Met needs every penny," said Mrs. Gimber. "These men and women are craftsmen, and they're very dedicated—you can see the quality in the costumes, which have to be built to last, and in such little things as swords or masks."

Some of this can be seen from the front of the house, but from there it's illusion. Backstage, it's the wood and the paint and the glue.

N O V E M B E R / D E C E M B E R						
30	1	2	3	4	5	5
Tosca	**Madama**	**Il trittico**	**Stravinsky**	**Carlo**	**Tosca**	**Il trittico**
Patanè;	**Butterfly**	*Campori;*	*Levine;*	**Bergonzi**	*Patanè;*	*Campori;*
Neblett,	*Fulton;*	*Savova,*	*Gelinas,*	**Gala**	*Neblett,*	*Savova,*
Carreras,	*Zylis-Gara,*	*Cruz-Romo,*	*Makarova,*		*Carreras,*	*Cruz-Romo,*
Milnes	*Kraft,*	*Craig,*	*Dowell;*		*Milnes*	*Craig,*
	Mauro,	*Taillon,*	*Bradley,*			*Taillon,*
	Sereni	*Moldoveanu,*	*Troyanos,*			*Moldoveanu,*
		Ciannella,	*Creech,*			*Ciannella,*
		MacNeil,	*Cassilly,*			*MacNeil,*
		Quilico	*Mazura,*			*Bacquier*
			Macurdy			

Homage

I t wasn't until the eleventh week that the first of the five new
productions at the Met took place: a triple bill of works by Igor
Stravinsky, to celebrate the hundredth anniversary (in 1982) of his
birth. The occasion was moderately gala, less because of the works
involved than because the noted English painter and set designer
David Hockney had been hired on the strength of his triumph
with the triple bill of French works (*Parade*) the previous year. (So
much for planning years in advance—at least as regards set designers.)

This was hardly the first time that a famous painter or sculptor
has been employed to set an opera or ballet, but the practice has
remained exceptional. Painters may know about form and color
(two qualities often lacking in stage design), but they are unused
to working in the theater, with its necessary compromises, or with
materials they do not understand. Further, they do not appreciate
the special qualities demanded of designers for repertory opera.

(In this, of course, they are joined by not a few journeymen stage designers who remain amateurs at their craft. And in a choice between two kinds of technical incompetents, why not pick the one who is at least a professional artist?) In his book *Richard Strauss: The Staging of His Operas and Ballets,* Rudolf Hartmann, as wise (if not as inspired) an operatic stage director as exists, refers to Salvador Dali's notorious set for *Salome* at Covent Garden: "Such set-designs (a more recent example is Chagall's set for the New York *Magic Flute*) have all had great individual charm, but are often unsatisfactory in that they are not readily adaptable to constantly changing spatial requirements, something which is essential in the theatre." To select one of Hartmann's examples: The second act of Strauss's *Arabella* is set at a ball. The impression of a room filled with people must exist, yet the plot requires an occasional intimacy within the scene.

The most effective sets, from the point of view of an opera's demands, are not necessarily those of stage-design geniuses. One of the most evocative (and apposite) sets in my Met memory was the central one of the duel between Lensky and Onegin in Tchaikovsky's *Eugene Onegin*. Rolf Gérard was hardly more than a gifted *routinier* in stage design, but Bing used him over and over because of his talents. In this simple setting, placed diagonally in a Russian winter landscape, Gérard distilled and congealed the force of the moment and the bleakness of the environment, while using the diagonal line of trees to parallel the diagonal along which Onegin and Lensky were separated. (The *Onegin* most recently on view at the Met is still ostensibly that of Gérard, but this scene has been modified through the years to a lesser visual effect.)

The major problem in hiring a noted painter, however, is not his inexpertise in the theater (Hockney, who has set operas at Glyndebourne, is no theater amateur) but his very power as an artist, which distorts the operatic entity. If the setting calls attention to itself beyond the first few minutes, it draws attention away from the opera itself. When the voices do this, they are at least fleshing out what the composer wrote. But the settings, while vital, are in almost all cases only meant to be secondary, elaborate as they may be.

The Met has generally not gone in for composer anniversary homages, except in an incidental way. But it was felt that Stravinsky was too important a figure in twentieth-century music to be ignored, particularly by a management that was trying to introduce major twentieth-century composers other than Richard Strauss and Puccini into the repertory.

Stravinsky, however, wrote very few works that could be classed as operas, and of those, very few (if any) are works best seen on a stage as large as the Met's. It is true that his longest opera, *The Rake's Progress,* had its American premiere at the Met during the Bing regime, but Levine feels that the opera is not suited for a large house.

The choice, therefore, fell on *Oedipus Rex,* the opera-oratorio of 1927, and the fairy-tale work *Le Rossignol* of 1914. The third work to fill out the evening was for a while undecided (Schoenberg's monodrama *Erwartung* was discussed), but finally Stravinsky's most historically famous work, *Le Sacre du printemps,* was selected to lead off.

This last choice was the most curious. Not because of the work's stature, which is enshrined, but because the Met wished, rightly, to present it in its original guise as a ballet. The fact is that *Le Sacre du printemps* has resisted successful ballet treatment from the beginning.

Now, this may not be a valid reason for a ballet company to ignore the work (though no less a master than Balanchine has maintained that it is unstageable), but it is doubly daunting for an opera company, for the ballet section of any opera company is almost by definition its weakest.

It is easy to see why this should be so. First of all, ballet and opera, while allied musico-dramatic forms, are quite separate aesthetics, and over the past fifty years they have developed along radically different paths. The audience for ballet is largely not the audience for opera, in New York, at least, and the adherents of each discipline tend to regard the other as an inferior art form. Similarly, dance has bred its own critics (e.g., Edwin Denby, John Percival, Walter Terry, Deborah Jowitt, Arlene Croce) who concentrate on that form alone.

Finally, though ballet was an integral part of opera at the outset and continued to be so (notably in France) until the late nineteenth century, opera companies have always treated it as the poor sister. Ballet performances are segregated into their own areas, in the intermissions between opera acts or in secondary slots within operas, like the ballets in *Aida* or the Dance of the Hours in *La Gioconda*. The growth in number and in importance of independent ballet companies over the past thirty years has only compounded the problem, for opera ballets have never been able to attract leading dancers, choreographers, or ballet masters on any long-term basis. There are too many opportunities elsewhere, before more knowledgeable and responsive audiences.

The Met, despite numerous fitful attempts, has never been able to develop more than a decent ballet corps, serviceable enough for the demands of the operas it presents, but hardly able to stand confidently on its own or to compete with other companies. (The management is now addressing that problem by having the ballet company perform on its own, outside the house, in the New York area; it also appeared at Jacob's Pillow in 1982. This undoubtedly serves to raise morale as well as performance standards.)

But the Met ballet had to stand on its own for *Le Sacre du printemps*, abetted by the choreography of Jean-Pierre Bonnefous, who was brought in when the original choreographer, Gray Veredon, withdrew in late summer. In the event, the focus shifted from the action onstage to the decorations provided by Hockney and the sounds emerging from the orchestra pit.

Those sounds emerged rather more fully than usual, for the movable pit had been raised to its highest level and surrounded by a glass screen so that the orchestra could be more clearly seen. The pit was filled to the brim with players.

John Dexter had suggested two unifying elements for the disparate triple bill: the figure of the circle and the use of masks. Hockney accepted these, and added a third: color contrasts. What resulted was striking in terms of stage pictures. And the most striking of all were the pictures devised for *Le Rossignol*. Yet, although *Rossignol* could be termed the "hit" of the evening, between the ballet *Sacre* and the austere, almost completely static *Oedipus Rex* (set in red and gold—reflecting the red and gold of the auditorium), it was in some ways the furthest from the pith of the story.

The story is simple: the nightingale is beautiful in song only because she is free. One cannot capture her song by mechanical means (as with the mechanical bird given to the Emperor), nor can one cage and discipline her (as the Emperor wishes to do). Without her song, however, the Emperor sickens unto death, for he has desperate need for her, and he is cured only when the nightingale returns of her own free will. The allegory is made obvious in the text, for the nightingale's song stands for music itself.

What Hockney did was to pile the trappings of his art onto the story. Circles were everywhere: in the orchestra pit, onstage, even reflected in the Fisherman's round hat. The various hues of blue, patterned after Chinese porcelain, were likewise ubiquitous, and provided a visual elegance of a sort not usually seen at the Met.

Yet the settings were distracting, not so much from the story as it unfolded as from the message behind the story. For it is the simple grace of music that grants, not a palliative, but the cure; and so any setting should seek to emphasize not complexity, but simplicity, and not the visual, but the aural: music itself. If Hockney's sets were too truly artistic to become, in a denigratory sense, the visual equivalent of the mechanical bird, they nonetheless partook of a kind of manufactured beauty specifically rejected by the story, and to that end they were deficient. The very artlessness-within-freely-produced-art that is the nightingale's song was given second place.*

It will be noted that the discussion of the evening has proceeded so far without reference to either dancers (Natalia Makarova, Anthony Dowell, and choreographer Sir Frederick Ashton were all

---

*It is true that Stravinsky himself felt that the even more elaborate original production (by Alexandre Benois) was the most beautiful of any of his works. The voice of the nightingale, however, was deeply embedded within the composer.

imported for *Rossignol*) or singers. And so it should have been, for Dexter himself stated that the evening was "a concerto for opera house and orchestra." (*Village Voice*, December 15, 1981) This shift of focus was a conscious plan of the management's, for it not only avoided the spotlighting of singers or dancers (despite the Makarova supporters in the audience) over the operas themselves, but utilized the talents of the corps de ballet and of many second-rank contract singers, thus improving morale. Opera, even at the Met, need not be viewed by starlight.

But if the spotlight here was focused on Hockney and the orchestra (which had, after all, to play one of the great virtuoso scores in symphonic literature), it was also kept focused on Stravinsky. The homage was genuine.

The very next night, December 4, saw another kind of homage—one more in keeping with the traditions of the house of Caruso. This was the celebration of the twenty-fifth anniversary of the Met debut of tenor Carlo Bergonzi.

The Met is understandably chary of these kinds of salutes, for no major opera house wants to show blatant favoritism for fear of losing other singers to fits of jealousy. (The celebrated case of James McCracken is an example. He was scheduled for a televised performance of *Tannhäuser*, but when the telecast was changed—for various reasons, one of them length—to *Otello*, McCracken was not asked to sing the title role. He felt that he was being deliberately slighted after a long career in the house, and took his voice elsewhere, breaking future contracts with the Met at considerable financial sacrifice to himself. Ironically, the Met will televise its *Tannhäuser* production in the spring of 1983.)

But if such tributes are rare, and usually coincide with either a longevity mark or outright retirement, they are welcomed by the opera buffs, for on such evenings some of the constraints are off the performances. The singer is allowed, for instance, to break character and bow after a big aria—usually a forbidden practice, though one now and then seen during the season. Vocalism is predominant.

This homage followed a pattern, once popular at the Met, of a "gala" of three acts from three different operas: a "highlights" format that attracts the marginal operagoer as well as the vocal buff. This evening's choices showed off the tenor voice, although the second portion of it, Act II of Verdi's *Un ballo in maschera* (not otherwise in this year's repertory), was given over to the sound of Luciano Pavarotti, in his seasonal debut. At one stage of the seasonal planning, the evening had been reserved for a Pavarotti concert; he is one of the very few artists guaranteed to sell out the Met for a solo appearance. But Pavarotti graciously deferred to his colleague and agreed to appear in one of his more famous roles.

Carlo Bergonzi, born in Parma in July 1924, has had a long career as a lyric-spinto tenor, including 246 performances at the Met through the 1981–82 season, from his debut as Radames in *Aida* on November 13, 1956. (Lyric spinto, in opera talk, means that he is essentially a lyric tenor, but has taken on more dramatic roles, such as Radames, but not the fully dramatic ones, such as Otello.) "Taste and restraint" (Harold Rosenthal's words in *The Concise Oxford Dictionary of Opera*) are often used in connection with Bergonzi's voice; and if he has never had the elegance of an Alfredo Kraus or the passionate refulgence of Giuseppe di Stefano at his best, he has had both intelligence and longevity. Although he is no actor onstage (in that respect he conforms to the public's idea of an operatic tenor), Bergonzi's easily produced voice, if more stolid and effortful than before, still defines the "Italian tenor" sound. His career has been a major one, and the homage was as well deserved as the tribute to Stravinsky the night before.

He appeared in the beginning of the second act of *Traviata*—the first item on the menu—to rapturous acclaim, and immediately bowed. James Levine, in the pit, saw to it that Bergonzi was given latitude for the expression of his big arias ("De' miei bollenti spiriti" from *Traviata* and "E lucevan le stelle" from the final act of *Tosca*, which concluded the performance). As the curtain fell on Bergonzi's rotund form, lying dead in the Roman morning light, the bravos began, and showers of cut-up paper descended from the higher reaches of the auditorium. (The Met has long banned the throwing of flowers onstage, because it is deemed hazardous to singers blinded by stage lights; but at least one bunch of flowers now and then manages to land at a singer's feet at curtain-call time.) The curtains parted once more, to reveal a podium and a lineup of artists and management. Levine gave way to Met president Frank Taplin, who presented a silver tray, and somehow even Luciano Pavarotti managed to speak—after giving the honoree an enormous bear hug. There was some disagreement as to whether the audience should or should not be invited to Bergonzi's restaurant in Busseto, Italy (the birthplace of Verdi). Bergonzi himself spoke only a few words of love, affection, and thanks.

			D E C E M B E R			
7	8	9	10	11	12	12
Stravinsky	**Il trittico**	**Rigoletto**	**Madama**	**Stravinsky**	**Il trittico**	**Rigoletto**
Levine;	*Campori;*	*Levine;*	**Butterfly**	*Levine;*	*Campori;*	*Levine;*
Gelinas,	*Savova,*	*Eda-Pierre,*	*Fulton;*	*Gelinas,*	*Savova,*	*Eda-Pierre,*
Makarova,	*Cruz-Romo,*	*Jones,*	*Craig,*	*Makarova,*	*Cruz-Romo,*	*Jones,*
Dowell;	*Malfitano,*	*Pavarotti,*	*Kraft,*	*Dowell;*	*Malfitano,*	*Pavarotti,*
Bradley,	*Berini,*	*Quilico,*	*Mauro,*	*Bradley,*	*Berini,*	*Quilico,*
Troyanos,	*Moldoveanu,*	*Berberian*	*Sereni*	*Troyanos,*	*Moldoveanu,*	*Berberian*
Creech,	*Ciannella,*			*Creech,*	*Creech,*	
Cassilly,	*MacNeil,*			*Cassilly,*	*Clark,*	
Mazura,	*Bacquier*			*Mazura,*	*Bacquier*	
Macurdy				*Macurdy*		

The Banyan Tree

The Bergonzi gala had been conducted by the music director, James Levine, and it so happened that the Wednesday, December 9, *Rigoletto* (with Pavarotti as the Duke), as well as the subsequent performances (one of them telecast), was being taken over by the music director from Giuseppe Patanè, who had conducted the first run of performances but had had to leave for Europe.

Ongoing complaints about any opera house, and certainly about the Met, often center not on what is being done, but on what is not. From the connoisseur of operas, the complaint is of works neglected or never heard; from the opera buff it is of singers not on the current roster or who have never been engaged. But always and pervasively, the complaint is about conductors.

Conductors at one time were, if not dispensable elements in the operatic picture, nonetheless minor figures ("No one ever paid a nickel . . ."), meant to keep the show in reasonable order and forward motion, but not—unless the opera was by Wagner—meant to get in the way of the singers. Whether it was Mahler or Toscanini who changed this view (both conducted at the Met) is less important than the fact that over the years it *has* been changed—to the chagrin of some vocal buffs, who still cling to the belief that the least intrusive conducting is the best conducting, and whose patron saint is Tullio Serafin. Certainly, if not from Toscanini's time then from that of the Second World War, when expatriate baton wielders of the eminence of Bruno Walter, Sir Thomas Beecham, Pierre Monteux, Fritz Reiner, and George Szell graced the Met's orchestra pit, there has been a consistent call for the Met to employ top conductors: a call that has gone largely unheeded in the Bing, Chapin, and Bliss regimes.

The standard response, at least of Bing and latterly of Bliss and Levine, has been that it is inordinately difficult to persuade a conductor of major stature to devote a large portion of his time, involving rehearsals and subsequently three or four weeks of performances, to a repertory opera house. Moreover, most top conductors insist on the right to choose their own casts and, in general, are unwilling to appear in anything but new productions. But whatever the arguments, the fact is that, of today's top level of conductors, neither Karajan nor Bernstein nor Abbado nor Solti nor Maazel nor Sir Colin Davis nor Mehta nor Barenboim nor Giulini nor Muti nor Ozawa nor Carlos Kleiber is presently at the Met, although over the years all but the last five have appeared there.

In this situation, two factors should be discussed: one that is almost always mentioned, and one that is almost never pointed out. To take the second first: an opera conductor is, and should be, a different conductor from a symphonic conductor. But to what extent this should be so is the crux of another ongoing and unanswerable debate.

Opera is by its very nature a combination of variables; it is a living, breathing entity that demands as much expansion in performance as control. This is particularly true because opera is dependent upon voices, and voices in their individuality should not be subject to the same rigidity of control as, for instance, the second violin section of an orchestra. That very flexibility which is the hallmark of great opera conductors counts for less in symphonic work (although it is evident in a symphony conductor's rapport with a soloist in a concerto); and although certain operas benefit from an iron and inexorable discipline from the pit, those very same operas can be made to sound straitjacketed and robotic in a way that a symphony does not.* To the connoisseur of opera, one of the greatest pleasures of a performance occurs when singer and conductor conjoin to make music, with neither dominating the other. A few seasons ago, for example, Julius Rudel (who knows his way around an opera pit) and Elena Obraztsova made out of Charlotte's letter scene from Massenet's *Werther* a continuously beautiful unfolding of music, word, and drama, with each participant responsive to the other's music making—and this in the context of a good, but hardly great, performance of the opera, in which Obraztsova was miscast.

The influence of Toscanini's recordings of opera has been, in this regard, pervasive. When Toscanini came to commit these operas to records, he was well over seventy, and the operas were performed as concert versions, without staging, with tight control. Whether or not these recordings are masterful as performances is not at issue: what is, is that they were almost certainly quite different from those he led when he was in the opera pits of Europe and South America at the end of the nineteenth and the beginning of the twentieth centuries. Yet their consciously applied unity of concept has pointed the way for many recorded performances of opera since then.

---

*One of the most thrilling and persuasive performances of Brahms's E-minor Symphony was that of the Dresden Staatskapelle Orchestra under Herbert Blomstedt—neither a top conductor nor a top orchestra—simply because of the discipline and élan of the East German group. The earlier performance (on the same night in the same hall—the Kennedy Center in Washington) of Schubert's "Great" C-major by the Vienna Philharmonic under Karl Böhm became, on reflection, pale in comparison. On the other hand, I found Sir Georg Solti's concert rendition of *Fidelio* in Carnegie Hall so machine-tooled that all life was squeezed out of it.

Again, the aim is not to argue against this unity (which can be evidenced at its most controlled in the crafted productions of opera that Herbert von Karajan has recently recorded for Deutsche Grammophon and EMI-Angel), but to note that this way of performing opera has too often been read back into the opera house, so that staged performances are considered primarily from a conductor's point of view. Thus, many opera lovers prefer listening to performances of a good, but not great, conductor who appreciates how operas should be performed—such as the Met's Giuseppe Patanè—to the work of a symphonist who rides roughshod over the opera in search of something else—such as the Met's Lawrence Foster.

The question is easier to define than to decide, though there is little doubt that the classic "singer's conductor" is today in deep disfavor, both with the critics and with the informed public. "In a time when there are no singers," says the Old Curmudgeon, "there is no need for singers' conductors." Yet, in disfavor or not, since operas can succeed on voice with secondary orchestral accompaniment, the type of conductor who would be denied the podium at symphony concerts is still in every opera pit the world over.

The other reason why the absence of major conductors at the Met is continuing cause for comment is precisely because the Met has a music director in James Levine. Sir Rudolf Bing never wanted a music director ("a post I frankly avoided because it seemed to me to divide responsibility that I thought should be the general manager's alone," he says in *5000 Nights at the Opera*), although he had several de facto advisors (Max Rudolf, Fritz Stiedry, George Schick, even, at times, Erich Leinsdorf and Dimitri Mitropoulos). But when Goeran Gentele assumed the general managership, he disagreed and appointed Rafael Kubelik. Schuyler Chapin appointed Levine to the post after Kubelik resigned, and today Levine is one of the most important figures in the administration of the Met.

Those who hoped that the presence of a music director would bring about the presence of other major conductors have been disappointed. With only a few exceptions, amounting to a handful of performances, major conductors have not been seen at the Met. This year, such figures would include Erich Leinsdorf, Bernard Haitink, and perhaps Andrew Davis, for a total of thirty-one performances, or roughly 14 percent of the season. As music director, Levine will conduct seventy-eight performances of ten evenings of opera, or roughly 37 percent.

Now, it is the opinion here that Levine is a major opera conductor—as some music directors of opera houses are not—and that as music director he should go into the pit a fair share of the time. But consider: these seventy-eight performances include three of the five new productions (in all three he is spelled for one performance or more by his assistant Jeffrey Tate), the opening night, and all gala events—the Bergonzi evening, the Verdi Requiem, and the Sunday-evening Troyanos/Domingo and Price/Horne concerts. He conducts all four televised operas (the two Sunday concerts will likewise be televised).

"Under the banyan tree nothing grows." The reasons why this saying is applicable to the Met are hard to pin down. Levine, when asked at press conferences* about the absence of major conductors—an almost inevitable question—is persuasive in his response. Levine is a particularly effective off-the-cuff speaker, managing to appear both open and frank in his discourse, and he is fully aware of his inborn ability to charm. He mentions the arguments given above as to time pressures, and notes that top conductors have their own jobs, which take a great deal of their time. He observes that the Met does not subscribe to the European habit (mentioned in the Leinsdorf interview) of having a major conductor prepare an opera, remain for the first four performances, and then turn it over to a house conductor.

On the other hand, there is the fact that, for whatever reason, the Met's music director has led most of the new productions there since his appointment. More significantly, of the new productions

---

*Or in the press; see the Arts and Leisure section of *The New York Times,* January 17, 1982, p. 21.

of operas by the musical giants of the core repertory—Mozart, Verdi, Wagner, and Puccini—Levine since 1976 has conducted eleven out of twelve.*

This activity may seem commendable when set against the news that Lorin Maazel, who takes over the Vienna Staatsoper in 1982, is contracted to go into the pit only forty times a year. Indeed, in the future the idea of a major conductor giving his audience the opportunity to hear his conception of operas from Mozart to Kurt Weill—with a consistently maturing and deepening approach to the music—may be looked back on as another golden age.

Two caveats should be given. One is that not infrequently Levine, who is only thirty-eight years old, is encountering these works either for the first time or after but a short previous acquaintance. The stricture of "on-the-job training" for conductors at the Met goes back well into the Bing years, and its results have not always been as negative as opinion holds (Schippers and Colin Davis managed quite well, Mehta and Maazel rather less so). Levine's undoubted gifts as an opera conductor have meant that, for him, the technical problems of the performance are relatively easy ones. Yet what Met audiences are being given amounts to a young man's view of the operas, and this view, however legitimate, has been balanced only by the maturity provided by Leinsdorf. If there are not many conductors with the ripe knowledge of a Walter or a Beecham around, there are nevertheless a few. But these men are more likely to want to conduct Mozart, Verdi, or Wagner than Puccini or Offenbach. Have they been foreclosed because there is a music director in the house?

The other caveat applies this year. Levine may well be the closest human equivalent to the perpetual motion machine; but can he, with even the best will, take on the range of styles and operas to the same effect for each work? Consider this fall's assignments:

---

*1976–77: *Lohengrin, La Bohème* (borrowed production); 1977–78: *Tannhäuser, Rigoletto;* 1978–79: *Don Carlo, Der fliegende Holländer* (borrowed production); 1979–80: *Die Entführung aus dem Serail, Manon Lescaut;* 1980–81: *La traviata;* 1981–82: *Così fan tutte, La Bohème. Un ballo in maschera* in 1979–80 is the exception.

Norma, Trittico, the three Stravinskys, *Bohème,* the reprise of *Rigoletto*—while looking forward to the new production of *Così.* Can he give each opera not only the physical but the spiritual attention it deserves? Particularly when, as music director, he must also concern himself with myriad administrative duties and public appearances vital to the running of the house; and he takes on outside concerts as well, such as the Music from Ravinia series at Alice Tully Hall.

When he was appointed music director, Levine said that one of his tasks would be to oversee not only the works he conducted, but the musical health of the entire organization, in terms of both musicological fidelity (Levine likes to give all operas in their complete form, without cuts, if possible) and preparation. Horror stories of singers put onstage without even the barest rehearsal were endemic in the Bing years—and indeed may be an inevitable concomitant to any repertory house not on a full stagione system. Yet this season, at least one leading soprano went onstage without rehearsal, and one conductor took over an operatic evening without rehearsal. Has Levine, in his zeal, spread himself too thin? What is the function of the music director: primarily administrative or primarily artistic? One suspects that Levine's response to the tasks confronting him are analogous to the mythical gourmand who, when presented with the first-class menu onboard the now legendary *France,* read it over thoughtfully, handed it back to the maître d'hôtel, and said, "Yes."

Before leaving the question of opera conducting, however, it is perhaps useful to look back at earlier Met history, if only for perspective, picking seasons not too close but not too distant. One of Bing's early seasons—1952–53—had nine conductors for approximately one hundred fifty performances, but only one—Fritz Reiner—who could be termed a top-level international conductor. He conducted three operas a total of twenty times. That would be the low point. In 1955–56, by contrast, there were twelve conductors for about the same number of performances as in 1952–53, and four could be classed as top—the old guard of Pierre Monteux (thirteen performances of three operas) and Bruno Walter (six *Magic Flutes*), Dimitri Mitropoulos (twenty-five performances of four operas), and Rudolf Kempe (nine performances of two operas). (Kempe may be assessed as marginal to the top class, but he was considered in that league by many operagoers.) In addition, Thomas Schippers conducted five *Don Pasquales*. This totals slightly more than a third of the performances.

For 1960–61, there were fifteen conductors for a slightly longer season of 177 performances. Of these, the old guard was represented by Stokowski (eight *Turandots*)—although he was hardly an old-guard *opera* conductor—and Karl Böhm (ten of three operas), plus Leinsdorf (twenty-nine of five), Solti (four *Tannhäusers*), and Schippers (seventeen of two operas). Again, the total is slightly more than a third of the season's performances. (Statistics such as these, of course, do not take into account the subjective factors: that "top" conductors may not conduct "top" performances, or that lesser conductors may.)

Now that there is a music director, the situation is different, both because the music director himself conducts a number of performances and because his presence and industry affect the quality of his orchestra. It is generally agreed that the Met orchestra today is playing, night after night, on a higher level of accomplishment than ever before. Richard Bonynge has called it the best opera orchestra in the world, and if that claim is highly debatable (given the merits of the Scala Orchestra and the Vienna Philharmonic, to name but two), the dramatic improvement of the Met orchestra is evident. If a music director should be held accountable for deficiencies, he must equally be given credit for success.

Levine's tenure as music director has granted Met-goers the opportunity to hear the maturing of a major conductor in a way that even the tenures of the music directors of the New York Philharmonic have not been able to match. There is no question that, today, the house of Caruso is not the house of Pavarotti or Domingo, but the house of Levine.

D E C E M B E R

14	15	16	17	18	19	19
La Bohème	**Rigoletto**	**Stravinsky**	**Madama**	**La Bohème**	**Rigoletto**	**Stravinsky**
Levine;	*Levine;*	*Tate;*	**Butterfly**	*Levine;*	*Levine;*	*Tate;*
Stratas,	*Eda-Pierre,*	*Gelinas,*	*Fulton;*	*Stratas,*	*Eda-Pierre,*	*Graves,*
Scotto,	*Jones,*	*Makarova,*	*Zylis-Gara,*	*Scotto,*	*Jones,*	*Makarova,*
Carreras,	*Pavarotti,*	*Dowell;*	*Kraft,*	*Carreras,*	*Alexander,*	*Dowell;*
Stilwell,	*Quilico,*	*Bradley,*	*Mauro,*	*Stilwell,*	*Quilico,*	*Bradley,*
Monk,	*Berberian*	*Quivar,*	*Sereni*	*Monk,*	*Berberian*	*Quivar,*
Morris		*Creech,*		*Morris*		*Creech,*
		Lewis,				*Lewis,*
		Mazura,				*Mazura,*
		Macurdy				*Macurdy*

Authenticity and
the Blockbuster

Puccini's *La Bohème* is one of the most popular operas of all time (it stands second on the Met list of most-performed operas, and is closing fast on *Aida*), and it is the one Puccini opera that Puccini haters grudgingly approve of. Its third act is arguably the most perfect (if hardly the greatest) act in all opera, in terms of mood, character portrayal in music, and the music itself: a unified whole, framed by the notes that begin and end it. As the Old Curmudgeon said, "With that act alone Puccini enters the Pantheon."

The Met's old production of *La Bohème*—sets by Rolf Gérard, original direction by the film director Joseph Mankiewicz—dates back to 1952, and caused a flutter by first being given in English. It was eventually retired, and a replacement was borrowed from the Chicago Lyric Opera; but it was evident that the Met needed one of its own. The company remedied the lack, in flamboyant style, by hiring Franco Zeffirelli, whose La Scala *Bohème* in 1963 was one of the most memorable opera productions of the postwar years.

Zeffirelli essentially enhanced and enlarged his earlier conception, giving the Met a lavish Christmas present (Acts I and II, after all, take place on Christmas Eve) that was rapturously received by the audience, if not by all the press. It will be a fixture in the house for many seasons.

Franco Zeffirelli tends to be associated with the spectacular in his stagings. Witness the world premiere of Samuel Barber's *Antony and Cleopatra* (which launched the Met's new house in 1966): the production almost willfully swallowed the music and the adaptation of Shakespeare's play whole. The Zeffirelli production of *Otello,* in Bing's last season, was similarly outsized, and was used as a touchstone for the kind of production the incoming management wished to avoid.

The spectacular, in the case of *La Bohème,* was represented by the second act, which sought to put onstage Christmas Eve in nineteenth-century Paris in all its variety: two levels of set, huddling buildings, lamp posts, carriages—and two hundred and eighty people. It was something out of Radio City Music Hall, and it was so teeming with variegated activity that the bustle effectively masked the behavior—and, indeed, the presence—of the bohemians.

It was, of course, a blockbuster of a stage picture. Was it Puccini's *Bohème?* Andrew Porter, in his review in *The New Yorker* (December 28, 1981), came up with an ingenious explanation: Zeffirelli was seeking a distancing of the passions and travails of the bohemians—and of the two principals—in the immensity of the city of Paris. This explanation, moreover, places *La Bohème* historically as a precursor of Charpentier's opera *Louise,* in which the city of Paris assumes a leading role in the "corruption" of the young seamstress. The setting of Acts I and IV of *Bohème* in a garret amidst the rooftops, so that it was seen as if from afar, contributed to this distancing, as did the crowded second act; and the gelid scene of Act III, with figures emerging out of a winter fog, again accentuated this loneliness.

La Bohème works as an opera and as an emotional theatrical experience because of Puccini's music and the passions of its characters. Their similarity to what we think of as bohemian life makes us believe in them. The passion of youth infects the opera and infects us, which is why *La Bohème* can be performed by young semiprofessionals or student singers and persuade us more than when it is sung by the top stars. Enrico Caruso and Nellie Melba may sing the first-act duet for the ages, but it is the unknowns who touch us in *Bohème*. (On television, Zeffirelli said he had never seen a bad production of *La Bohème*. Although he doubtless overstated the case, his point is well made.)

Zeffirelli's production tacitly admits that a *Bohème* at the Met, because of the size of the stage and the singers' practiced professionalism, can never achieve this immediacy and authenticity of youth. Rather than creating a simulacrum, then, Zeffirelli has sought to provide compensation by shifting the authenticity from youth and immaturity to the feel of a big city. Innocence, as John Rockwell noted in his *New York Times* review (December 15 and 16, 1981), has been lost; but can innocence ever be incarnated by the kind of singers employed by the Met?

Zeffirelli's greatest contribution to stagecraft is not his tendency to gigantism but his evocation of mood. In this he is unrivaled. Indeed, it is his manipulation of emotion through stage lighting and through subtle genre touches such as smoke curling from rooftop chimneys that best define him as a stage director—more so than his handling of character, which is appropriate, often dramatically vivid, but rarely insightful.

Zeffirelli's control of mood through lighting can be seen in his many films and is at its finest in the opera house when he is on hand to oversee the lighting board. Act III of *La Bohème*, with the figures becoming three-dimensional as they materialized out of an early-morning winter fog, was magical and very beautiful. It played, not incidentally, directly to the strengths of the house, in terms of the Met's resources.

(The telecast of *La Bohème* on January 20 most clearly demonstrated the differences between seeing the opera at the Met and seeing it on the screen. The teeming Act II "city of Paris" was completely lost, with the figures reduced to raisins in a rice pudding, and none of the bustle and energy of the whole transmitted. The sense of event was gone. The close-ups, moreover, distracted from rather than built up the progress of the act. Similarly, Act III had little of the magic it created in the house, because the subtleties of the lighting did not come across, although the snowfall—augmented for television—did register. The singers looked their parts, since casting for type rather than for voice works well on television. Teresa Stratas's Mimi seemed properly consumptive, while José Carreras's Rodolfo looked like a young—and at least semi-starving—bohemian. Yet the televised performance, whatever else it did, did not project the strengths of Zeffirelli's ideas, simply because those ideas were not designed for television. The performance "worked" because it was *La Bohème*.)

If the singers looked their parts, and the setting was authentically that of nineteenth-century Paris . . . what about the voices? Were they also authentic?

The question of vocal authenticity was once considered vital to opera. Italians are best for Italian opera; Germans for German; French for French. There was a style appropriate for each genre, and that style could be properly expressed only by singers trained in the native and specialized techniques.

This thinking has changed. The internationalization of casts, particularly after the Second World War, meant that a sort of generalized style, loosely based on the Italian model, became the norm, with pockets of resistance in the German repertory (such as the rough-grained, hectoring vocal declamation of Wagner, which has become known in the trade as "the Bayreuth bark") and, increasingly rarely, in the French—and, of course, the individual style of singers coming from behind the Iron Curtain. Though audiences at a large international house like the Met still do not want to hear German-trained tenors taking on Verdi, a neutral, all-purpose tenor such as the Swedish-Russian Nicolai Gedda can essay some Verdi roles. And there has been a sufficient homogenization to permit almost any kind of cross-national casting, especially since the arrival of great numbers of American and, latterly, English singers. Only the most specialized vocal buffs now talk of authenticity of style when it comes to casting, and even they are more concerned with vocal production and individuality of expression than with accuracy of style.

The fact is that there is no longer a single, unified national style of singing (except, perhaps, behind the Iron Curtain). Wagner himself wanted, but rarely got, an Italianate singing style for his operas. Today, the ubiquity of what could be termed the "Verdi bark"—the punching out of the high notes in a melodramatic way at the expense of the vocal line—has led to a generation of singers who cannot provide the ongoing musical phrasing integral to bel canto. Thus, many Italian-trained singers can no longer sing Italian opera in an "authentic" way. When a quintessentially French opera such as Massenet's *Werther* can be recorded in versions containing singers from the United States, Russia, Sweden, Italy, England, and Spain, one is no longer involved with questions of authenticity of style, except in the loosest way.

The same is true of conductors. Italian opera today is the province not of Italian conductors, but of such international stars as Bernstein, Solti, Levine, Karajan, and Colin Davis. Do Abbado and Muti bring to Italian opera that specialized style which Monteux and Ansermet once brought to French opera?

The *Bohème* cast included one Italian (Renata Scotto) in a principal role, one Spaniard (Carreras), a Canadian (Stratas), and a clutch of Americans, and was conducted by an American, yet no one objected to its lack of Italian flavor. What has now become more important than a national style is *Fach*—whether a singer is right for a role—and this transcends national boundaries. Nilsson's *Fach* was Wagner and Richard Strauss; one listened to her as Aida or Tosca because she was Birgit Nilsson.

There is another question that lies behind this production of *La Bohème*. The production itself is a glittering achievement, guaranteed to appeal to subscribers and ticket buyers, and guaranteed to last in the repertory. It is flexible enough, as a playing space and as a traditional view, to accommodate a variety of singers over the years. Is that, and should that be, its justification?

Samuel Lipman, music critic for *Commentary*, sees the production as symbolic of the Met's general stance. Although he loves the opera, he feels that lavishing this amount of money (said to be seven hundred and fifty thousand dollars) on it only highlights the safe, conservative attitude of the house.

"The Met lacks any willingness to stand failure," he said to me. "And in an artistic endeavor there is no way out of risks. The Met manages to change just enough so that no change is noted, but just enough so that the result does not appear dated."

If a repertory house should have the courage to dare, and to dare to fail, the Met has not recently met that challenge, except in regard to operas marginal to the core repertory. Lipman admired the highly controversial Jean-Pierre Ponnelle production of *Der fliegende Holländer* of a few seasons back, simply because it dared to be different in its basic conception (the whole opera was seen from the point of view of one of the minor characters).

The Met, however, confidently pursues the middle way, and in so doing has continued its separation from any dynamic of a creative artistic force. It is simply uninterested in that role. *La Bohème* produced by Zeffirelli, whatever its merits, may be more Zeffirelli than Puccini, or more spectacle than intimate genre opera. But it is exactly what the management ordered.

		D E C E M B E R				
21	22	23	24	25	26	26
Hansel and Gretel	**Madama Butterfly**	**Stravinsky**	**La Bohème**	**Hansel and Gretel**	**Madama Butterfly**	**Hansel and Gretel**
Woitach;	*Fulton;*	*Levine;*	*Levine;*	*Woitach;*	*Fulton;*	*Woitach;*
Blegen,	*Zylis-Gara,*	*Graves,*	*Stratas,*	*Blegen,*	*Zylis-Gara,*	*Robinson,*
Troyanos,	*Kraft,*	*Makarova,*	*Scotto,*	*Troyanos,*	*Kraft,*	*Bybee,*
Elias,	*Mauro,*	*Dowell;*	*Mauro,*	*Elias,*	*Mauro,*	*Elias,*
Devlin	*Elvira*	*Bradley,*	*Stilwell,*	*Devlin*	*Elvira*	*Thompson*
		Troyanos,	*Sereni,*			
		Creech,	*Morris*			
		Cassilly,				
		Mazura,				
		Macurdy				

Christmas and "Hansel and Gretel"

C hristmas is traditionally a slow time artistically at the Met. The house this year was decorated with small trees, deciduous and evergreen and festooned with tiny lights, and the grand staircase and the balconies were draped in bottle-green cloth trimmed with gold braid, with a gold-braid emblem of an encircled "M" at the center as one entered. It was more appropriate, one felt, for the state funeral of James Bond's superior than for the Nativity.

On December 21 Humperdinck's *Hansel and Gretel* (in English) entered the repertory for eight performances at reduced prices. It did not, except in the general sense, enter the repertory, for all of the performances were non-subscription.

The Met has long wanted a "Christmas show" as unfailingly successful as the New York City Ballet's *Nutcracker*. *Hansel and Gretel* is, despite its lack of Christmas connections, a traditionally safe choice. But, for all the magic and the sentiment of the opera and its production, with its flying angels, pirouetting mushrooms, and its cookie house that rises from the ground, and for all the antics of the Witch (this time cast with a woman rather than with the alternate character tenor), *Hansel,* if orchestrally solidly crafted (Humperdinck learned his lessons well at the feet of Wagner), has none of the sustained magic of the Tchaikovsky ballet. The musty aura of "children's opera" still clings to the work, and will always do so, to the opera's detriment.

The Met's production, which dates from 1967, has recently been trotted out at Christmas with an assortment of young singers and veterans—and this year a house conductor. It is performed not for its own sake, but because it coincides in some oblique way with the season and can be used as an enticement, less to children than to adults who have young ones to be amused over the holidays. The perfunctory and at times slipshod nature of the presentation only underlines the commercial attitude of the event.

Nowhere is the lack of programmatic daring of the Met more clearly evident, for there exist several operas that better fit the Christmas season, not least Thea Musgrave's recently composed (1979) and charming *A Christmas Carol.* But there is safety in *Hansel,* even though it appeals only to the youngest in the audience, and even though it has worn out its welcome at the box office through gross overexposure.

D E C E M B E R / J A N U A R Y

28	29	30	31	1	2	2
Stravinsky	**La Bohème**	**Hansel**	**Madama**	**Hansel**	**Stravinsky**	**La Bohème**
Levine;	*Levine;*	**and Gretel**	**Butterfly**	**and Gretel**	*Levine;*	*Levine;*
Graves,	*Stratas,*	*Woitach;*	*Fulton;*	*Woitach;*	*Graves,*	*Stratas,*
Makarova,	*Scotto,*	*Blegen,*	*Zylis-Gara,*	*Blegen,*	*Makarova,*	*Scotto,*
Dowell;	*Mauro,*	*Troyanos,*	*Kraft,*	*Bybee,*	*Dowell;*	*Carreras,*
Bradley,	*Stilwell,*	*Elias,*	*Mauro,*	*Elias,*	*Bradley,*	*Stilwell,*
Troyanos,	*Sereni,*	*Devlin*	*Elvira*	*Devlin*	*Troyanos,*	*Monk,*
Creech,	*Morris*				*Creech,*	*Morris*
Lewis,					*Lewis,*	
Mazura,					*Mazura,*	
Macurdy					*Macurdy*	

The Archives

A s this book has already shown, any consideration of one year at the Metropolitan Opera includes its relationship with the past. The Met is approaching its centennial season—not long in terms of La Scala, but long enough when it is realized that many opera companies were never entities such as they are today, but the creations of impresarios who rented the playing spaces, which happened to be the opera houses. The history of Covent Garden, for example, is the history of various companies, not of a single "Covent Garden Opera"—and that until after World War II. The Met's past is one of a similarly checkered relationship between its general managers and the Metropolitan Opera and Real Estate Company (well documented in Irving Kolodin's history of the Met). But it is safe to say that the house's continuity of performances over the seasons represents a signal artistic achievement, and goes a long way to justify the obsessional efforts of so many in management and on the board to raise enough monies to continue at the same stand in much the same way.

This sense of history is, unfortunately, not immediately present to most Met operagoers entering the house for a night at the opera. In the old house, those coming in the Broadway doors were greeted by the gold bust of Enrico Caruso, and the walls of the house were lined with portraits, busts, and memorabilia of the famous singers and conductors who performed there (plus a few more: the portrait of Richard Strauss conducting an opera was misleading; he never conducted at the Met). Today, however, the Caruso bust is relegated to the lower level, behind a bar, and the rest of the portraits reside in the gallery on the same level, effectively invisible to most of the audience unless they check their coats. The memorabilia vitrines are on the box level, while the upper reaches of the house are bare of memories (Maillol and Lehmbruck statues, whatever their artistic merit, have no relation to the Met). If you are a member of the Metropolitan Opera Guild, you can view a portrait of Mrs. Belmont in the Guild-members-only Belmont Room; if you are a member of the Metropolitan Opera Club, you can see a bust of longtime club member Giovanni Martinelli; and if you want a drink of water, you can quaff at the Ezio Pinza memorial fountains throughout the house.

And yet the Met, more than most performing companies, has managed to preserve its past, less through its iconography than through the Metropolitan Opera Archives. These archives are extensive; they are, thankfully, in good hands; and they constitute a vital and seldom-mentioned resource.

The archives can be broken down into several parts. Most obviously, there are the written archives of the company. Then there are the iconographic archives mentioned above, and the costume archives of famous singers, from a time when each singer wore his or her own costume and there was no sense of an overall costume design concept. The Met, luckily, owns a fine collection of costumes of Kirsten Flagstad and Enrico Caruso, two of its most celebrated stars. Finally, there are the audio archives of the company.

The lasting credit for the preservation and maintenance of the Met's written archives is owing to one volunteer, Mrs. John DeWitt

Peltz. Mary Ellis Peltz was as single-minded and tenacious in her love of the Met as her good friend Mrs. Belmont. Robert Tuggle, the recently appointed successor to Mrs. Peltz as archivist, is similarly dedicated.

"The crucial time," he said, "was when the company moved to Lincoln Center. Mrs. Peltz had the files in such good order that they were easily able to be transferred. Her work over the years has been invaluable."

The amazing fact is that, although Tuggle constantly receives telephone calls about specific questions (and mostly about singers), few people have ever made extensive use of this treasure trove of information about opera and opera performance. Mrs. Peltz's cross-indexing of operas and artists is in itself a mine of information, but it is only one small part of what is contained in the archives.

Also included are the correspondence of general managers from Gatti to the present, union negotiations from 1920 onward, programs going back to 1883, and pressbooks containing reviews from newspapers dating back to 1903–04. These last are fascinating, as in those days New York had a number of newspapers and journals, and all of them wrote about Met performances—and not just the first ones; in some cases every performance was covered.

There are cash books and journals back to 1883, pay books from 1896, and box-office and salary records.

For instance, for the 1915 season, each payment to Enrico Caruso is carefully documented by day and role. (He received $2,500 per performance up to forty performances and $2,000 thereafter.) A letter from the Victor Talking Machine Company lists Caruso's royalties from records in 1915 as an aggregate of $145,207.

One of the most famous performances in Met history took place on Saturday afternoon, February 2, 1935, when the unknown Kirsten Flagstad made her debut as Sieglinde in *Die Walküre*. The files trace the route she took to the Met stage. Frida Leider, the Met's leading Wagnerian soprano, had decided not to return; but instead of informing the management of her decision, she chose to dither about a clause in her contract calling for her to tour. Eric Simon, the Met's European contact, rightly guessed that Leider was using this ploy to cancel, and the name of a little-known Norwegian singing at that time at Bayreuth came up. Edward Ziegler, Gatti's assistant, carried on the correspondence with Simon while Gatti was abroad and arranged for Flagstad to meet Gatti and his chief conductor, Artur Bodanzky, in St. Moritz for an audition on August 22 (her travel expenses to be paid—second class!). Simon wrote Ziegler on August 11, 1934, giving Flagstad's repertory, which did not include Brünnhilde. (In another letter to Bodanzsky, he did say that she had the three Brünnhilde roles ready for performance.)

Gatti wrote to Ziegler on September 6: "She made an excellent impression and I have engaged her. . . . This will mean a substantial economy over the Leider contract." It certainly would: Leider was getting $710 per performance (compare that in the Depression economy to Caruso's salary twenty years earlier!), whereas the contract Flagstad signed was settled at $550 per week, with ship fare for herself and her husband. (Simon had suggested to Flagstad to ask for $500 a week, with two performances maximum per week, and to Bodanzky that she be paid $600 weekly; hence the compromise figure of $550.)

During the fall Gatti, through Ziegler, wrote Simon that in addition to her Wagnerian roles Flagstad should prepare the Marschallin in *Der Rosenkavalier*, a role she had never sung. "It is not a long part," wrote Ziegler, "as it consists practically of one act and a trio. . . ." Simon, on October 12, replied that Flagstad refused, and the management did not insist.

As well it should not have, for after the February 2 Sieglinde, Flagstad proceeded, imperturbably, to sing Isolde four nights later, the *Walküre* Brünnhilde on February 15, the *Götterdämmerung* Brünnhilde on February 28, Elisabeth in *Tannhäuser* on March 15, Elsa in *Lohengrin* on March 18, and Kundry in *Parsifal* on April 17. Those were really the days of the singer's house!

Also on file in the archives are singers' contracts and some correspondence, from Gatti's time to the present, an extensive photograph collection of singers (strongest for the last fifty years), and photographs and stage plans of operas.

One of the banes of operatic performance, for the impresario as well as the audience, is cancellation through indisposition. There is a handwritten note from Olive Fremstad (whom Michael Scott in *The Record of Singing* calls "the most naturally endowed of the great Wagnerian sopranos active at the turn of the century" and who was fictionally rendered in Willa Cather's novel *The Song of the Lark*) pinned to a doctor's note, reading: "I am not better this morning and I must therefore abide by my doctor's order, i.e., not to sing this week. I should not have sung last Saturday. Too bad I did so because it will only delay the recovery." The role she sang that Saturday in December 1911 was the title role of Gluck's *Armide* under Toscanini.

Otto Kahn was a voluminous letter writer to Gatti and oversaw the house as a personal extension of his home. On one occasion, he wrote Gatti about a complaint he had received from an operagoer friend who had been slighted by the Met's carriage call man in preference to someone else who had tipped him. Kahn wrote, "[The carriage call man] must treat everyone alike whether they give him tips or not. These little matters are of the utmost importance in creating public sentiment. Even the best of performances will not make us friends if people are not treated courteously and fairly at the box office and everywhere else."

Finally, there is a telegram to Rudolf Bing in 1958, after Callas walked out on the Met, of a kind probably seen all too often nowadays in this media-conscious world. It announces the availability of a woman who possesses "the world's highest coloratura voice" and who is "operatic ambassadress to the Western world." Her voice, Bing is assured, is "greater than Callas's" and "in its absolute purity and splendor of control will make her name paramount among the great prima donnas of our day."

Some of the less-in-demand files are currently being transferred to the warehouse in New Jersey, although Tuggle wants to keep as many as possible (as well as the costume inventory) in the house, either for easy reference or for safekeeping. "Anything else we can get at with a couple of days' notice."

One advantage of the Met's drive for financial stability is that it can afford to pay for what once was a volunteer effort. A contribution to the archives has meant that the position of archivist is now salaried (although Tuggle still uses volunteers), and monies are currently being sought for the future preservation of the records.

"My first priority would be to microfilm the pressbooks, which are deteriorating," said Tuggle. (Since this interview, the microfilming has begun.) "After that, I would like to microfilm the programs themselves and the correspondence, and put Mrs. Peltz's index on a computer. That index, by the way, is in one respect incomplete. It does not include the tour performances until about five years ago, or the performances of ballet in the house. That would have to be added."

Concurrent with these efforts to facilitate research is the preparation of exhibits for in-house use or for traveling shows. Finally, Tuggle would like to see the publication of certain of the files.

One such publication has long been an outstanding achievement of the Metropolitan Opera Guild. This is the Metropolitan Opera Annals, giving complete casts of all performances, originally compiled by William H. Seltsam and updated to 1976 by Gerald Fitzgerald. The first two volumes of the Annals have for several years been out of print and fetch a commanding price when found. Tuggle has put first priority on reprinting them, correcting the errors, and adding certain facts such as the names of directors, designers, dancers, and choreographers. (It is indicative of the relative unimportance of these people that they were not deemed significant enough to be included. How opera, the unchangeable, has changed!) Gerald Fitzgerald and Jean Uppman are currently at work on the project, using paybooks to check whether a singer in fact sang as scheduled; and though it is now impossible to have the reprint (in two volumes) ready in time for the centennial season, it is expected to be available shortly thereafter.

"We exist for those people who want to know more rather than less," said Tuggle. The Met archives are indeed among the most complete records—and probably the best catalogued—of any such archives, anywhere. (Their condition stands in stark contrast, for instance, to the lamentable state of the archives of the New York Philharmonic.)

The audio archives can be properly divided into two parts: one under Met control and one a historical document made at the old Metropolitan Opera House. In the early twentieth century Lionel Mapleson, the Met's librarian, made a series of recordings of excerpts from actual in-house performances on Edison cylinders from the catwalk of the Met. These invaluable documents of how singers sounded then *in performance* were eventually acquired (in part) by Seltsam and are now in the Rodgers and Hammerstein Archives of the New York Public Library at Lincoln Center.* It is expected that recordings made from these cylinders will be issued by the library during the Met centennial. Despite the rudimentary sound, these documents are of priceless value. They feature performances by artists who never or only rarely recorded in the studio, and are the earliest documentation we have of artists in performance.

The Met owns all its broadcasts since 1950, and a good number of the pre-1950 broadcasts. (These are in the process of being transferred to cassette tape at the Rodgers and Hammerstein Archives.) And at the suggestion and originally under the direction of the Johnson Associates and then the late Dario Soria, they form the basis of a reissue program of famous performances of the past. The 1982 issue, produced by Mrs. Dario Soria and David Hamilton, is one of the legendary Ljuba Welitsch/Fritz Reiner performances of Strauss's *Salome*, coupled with an Astrid Varnay/Reiner *Elektra*.

It is becoming increasingly evident that recordings such as this series are of historical importance, for they present the operas as

---

*An article on the Mapleson cylinders, their history and contents, can be found in the *Journal of the Association for Recorded Sound Collections* 12:3 (1981), pp. 5–20.

they were performed at that time, with certain performance practices and cuts that give us an idea of how opera has changed. And they give the public an opportunity to hear singers in roles they never recorded commercially (e.g., Jussi Bjoerling's Riccardo in *Un ballo in maschera*). David Hamilton, who is currently working on the Met's centennial audio release program, is not alone in believing that these recordings will become as valuable a research tool as scores and written documents. In this way, the Met's past becomes an integral part of its present and its future.

J A N U A R Y

4	5	6	7	8	9	9
Tannhäuser	**Hansel**	**La Bohème**	**Hansel**	**Tannhäuser**	**Hansel**	**La Bohème**
Levine;	**and Gretel**	*Levine;*	**and Gretel**	*Levine;*	**and Gretel**	*Levine;*
Rysanek,	*Woitach;*	*Stratas,*	*Woitach;*	*Rysanek,*	*Woitach;*	*Stratas,*
Dunn,	*Blegen,*	*Scotto,*	*Blegen,*	*Dunn,*	*Blegen,*	*Scotto,*
Cassilly,	*Troyanos,*	*Carreras,*	*Troyanos,*	*Cassilly,*	*Troyanos,*	*Carreras,*
Weikl,	*Chookasian,*	*Stilwell,*	*Chookasian,*	*Weikl,*	*Chookasian,*	*Stilwell,*
Estes	*Devlin*	*Sereni,*	*Devlin*	*Estes*	*Devlin*	*Monk,*
		Morris				*Morris*

In the Gods

The first week of the new year opened with the season's first performance of Wagner's early opera *Tannhäuser*. This production, new in 1977–78, has been one of the most acclaimed of the present management's offerings and is certainly one of Levine's special projects, in the sense that for each revival he seeks to make it better. He told me, rather proudly, that though the original director, Otto Schenk, had not been on hand to restage it this season, he had nonetheless seen it and had told Levine that it was better now than it had been at its 1977 premiere. This, Levine said Schenk told him, was unknown in Europe, where productions often deteriorate rapidly—so rapidly that the original director rarely wants to see what has happened since he left.

I spent that first night in the gods. "The gods" is the Family Circle (497 seats)—more particularly, the back of the Family Circle—and if it is not a secret to opera buffs, it is one of the better-kept secrets from the public at large. A seat in the gods is one of the best bargains in music.

The media like to dramatize the high cost of operagoing by citing the cost of an orchestra seat; and, indeed, there are proportionally more higher-cost tickets available for single sale than tickets in the lower price categories (for seats that are higher in the house). Yet, in early December, I went to the box office and purchased a seat on the aisle three rows from the back of the Family Circle for ten dollars. For this, I got a full view of the stage, except for the second level of the sets; and, more to the point, I got some of the best sound in the entire house.

This sound, which is acoustician Cyril Harris's eternal legacy to the financially less fortunate, is the secret. I have little doubt that the Met could sell most, if not all, of the Family Circle to subscribers (as it does sell a considerable portion of it) because of that factor alone.

The sound in the gods has amazing presence—far more presence than in the "critics' seats" in the orchestra—an extremely good balance of orchestra and voice, and a combination of ideal individuality of timbre and instrument with a totality of tone. It is true that in certain sections (well known to the regulars) the sound does have its oddities—the castanets in the Venusberg bacchanale and the triangle in Act II were so "live" they seemed ten feet away. But there was a general feeling that one was participating directly in the operatic event. The clarity of Richard Cassilly's German diction, as Tannhäuser, was such that one could have taken down the text as dictation; and the special qualities of each voice were always evident. Similarly, the orchestral sound had body and power, yet single instruments such as the flute and clarinet could be clearly heard in their solo passages. The bass sound of the cellos, in that famous homage to chromaticism, Wolfram's "evening star" aria, underpinned Bernd Weikl's singing while contributing a carpet of sensuous beauty; and it was one of a host of such musical pleasures.

One of the characteristics of the sound in the new Met as opposed to the old is that a really big voice does not have the same physical presence it did in the Thirty-ninth Street house, at least in the Dress Circle or the Balcony. But under the overhang in the back reaches of the Family Circle, big voices like Cassilly's or Mignon Dunn's reacquire that presence, to the extent of an almost palpable push.

On the other hand, one of the features of the Lincoln Center house has always been its extreme kindness to lighter voices. Kathleen Battle's exquisite singing of the Shepherd's unaccompanied music in the second scene of Act I (I cannot imagine that role better sung) spun and glittered with a pristine, crystalline beauty enhanced by its exact intonation. Many debuting singers do not realize this and try to force their voices for the spaces of the Met. It is needless: a light soprano with adequate projection, or a lighter tenor, such as Nicolai Gedda, makes a quite impressive effect. Operas calling for lighter voices, such as *Ariadne auf Naxos*, *Così fan tutte*, or even *Der Rosenkavalier*, sound simply gorgeous in the upper reaches of the house; and many opera buffs who do not particularly want to see the work (or who have seen the production a few times before) buy seats along the side of the balcony, next to the score desks, and enjoy.

"But I sit in the orchestra because I want to *see* the opera," ripostes a longtime subscriber. And, indeed, if that is the prime criterion, one is better off downstairs, for even with a full view of the stage, sitting in the Family Circle reduces the singers to lilliputians, and one is well advised to bring a good pair of binoculars.

The audience upstairs is multifaceted and multilingual. I heard six languages spoken—American, English, Chinese, German, Spanish, and French—some by subscribers, some by visitors. The old immigrant populations that stuffed the gods with people wanting to hear the tunes from the homeland are gone, replaced by their grandsons and granddaughters. Although the audience contains older people and the hardcore opera buffs (who congregate among themselves and trade signed publicity photos of singers the way others would trade baseball cards), the remarkable aspect of the upstairs crowd is the youth of so much of it, from boy-and-girl couples to the homosexuals who are ever in attendance.

Philip, the rotund Italian, was behind the bar, and while dispensing wine, liquor, and soft drinks ("*Pepsi*-Cola—I tell them that so they know what they're getting"), he greeted the regulars who came up to wish him Happy New Year and shook their hands. He automatically set up the bourbon and soda for one customer. Philip comes in every day from his home in the Rockaways, on the filthy subway, and was this night happy, because the opera was by Wagner—"I'm the man of Italian descent who likes Wagner." This was his last night at the upstairs bar; under union rules he is rotated every two weeks, first to the Patrons Bar in the Board Room and then, as he put it, "to Caruso"—i.e., to the bar in front of the Caruso bust on the lower level. "I'll see you there," said one subscriber.

The spirit of camaraderie between the subscribers and the house staff is particularly evidenced in the subscribers' relationship with the ushers. Bob Brann, who works the left-hand orchestra aisle, is a long-time regular; in the first weeks of the season he spends time renewing acquaintance with his subscribers, and in the last weeks he wishes them all a good summer.

This camaraderie, an integral part of the "Met family" ambience consciously fostered by the management, is a facet of Met-going that is rarely mentioned in the press; yet it is very important. A subscriber-oriented house, with many people coming ten to fifteen times during the season, has in some sense become a substitute for the nineteenth-century private club—a place to which one can repair and find friendly faces and, not incidentally, an evening of music and spectacle. Subscription evenings and matinees are alive with conversations among adjacent seat holders, who may not see each other at any other time, but who discuss births, deaths, and rites of passage. And in the closing weeks of the seasons the ushers are often remembered financially. One box holder put it this way: "I have my table reserved in the Grand Tier restaurant, and I invite friends. When I arrive at the opera house at six o'clock I turn off the outside world. I have a good dinner and see an opera—sometimes it's good and sometimes it's not, but that really doesn't matter as long as it's entertaining. In the intermissions, I return to my table and have dessert, coffee, maybe champagne. Yes, it costs me a lot, but it's worth it."

This communal spirit has some intriguing side effects. A few years ago, one performance was bedeviled with cancellations and substitutions, and the cover for the lead soprano role was unavailable. A last-minute substitute was found, and she gave a performance that was by most standards inadequate, and by Met standards a scandal. One would have thought that subscribers would protest, but those to whom I spoke felt the opposite—that in this time of the Met's trial one had to rally round and support her. The family stood together.

The ramifications of this are not difficult to perceive. If, on the surface, the reality of an audience largely composed of regulars can justify a certain adventurousness in programming without risking empty houses, too much adventurousness can lead to subscriber cancellations. Thus the pressure is constant to program for the benefit of the middlebrow, while slipping in a few novelties per season. This year the Stravinsky evening was considered "boring" by some subscribers (judging from those to whom I spoke and those who left during its course), but only a few subscription series contained it, and those who were bored were willing to pay what it cost to hear the more popular operas on the series. If, however, there are too many such items, subscribers may become single-ticket buyers or abandon the house altogether for more conservative venues, much as subscribers to the New York Philharmonic during the Boulez years switched to the more comfortable programming of the visiting Philadelphia Orchestra or Boston Symphony.

The management consciously relies on habit as much as on this family spirit, which is equally consciously used as a bargaining tool by the unions at contract time, since the Met has found from experience that after a strike it loses a portion of its subscribers who "get out of the habit."

The strictly musical factor, however, should not be underestimated in this evaluation. Even if a majority of the subscribers are unable to hear the differences between singers and conductors, and demand the visual to a greater degree than do the opera buffs, the naked emotional impact of a good deal of the nineteenth-century repertory provides an empathetic bond at once compelling and distinct from that granted by either movies or the hyperactive and often badly amplified Broadway musicals, and it provides an immediacy of human contact not satisfied by home entertainment. There are today dozens of recordings of the standard operas (and there will soon be dozens of videodiscs and videotapes), any one of which will provide a more ideal operatic experience than the average repertory night at the Met. But still, each night thousands of operagoers prefer to spend the money to be in the house, with all the ancillary difficulties of travel and expense that it entails.

On the night of *Tannhäuser*, the atmosphere in the gods was electric. Wagner was returning to the house—a Wagner evening has always been special, both because of the musical spells woven by the Old Magician and because of the success of his campaign to separate his operas from the common run—in a production that has been deemed one of the Met's strongest (and most traditional). There is usually less coughing and rustling in the upper reaches of the house, and fewer people leave during the last act. Attention is paid, to the disgruntlement of one standee, who said, half jokingly, half seriously, to the patrons: "Why don't you people go home so that we can sit down?" (Family Circle standing room is the cheapest ticket with a view of the stage: the score desks are cheaper, but have no view.) A long, long way away, the tale of the man torn between sensuality and piety unfolded, and one could see the pinpoint of light from the closed-circuit television receiver in the prompter's box. The music from the orchestra pit and then from the stage welled up and was concentrated by the overhanging gold roof. As the Inveterate Opera Buff once put it, "It's as good a reason as any to be alive."

J	A	N	U	A	R	Y	
11	12	13	14	15	16	16	
Luisa	**Tannhäuser**	**La Bohème**	**Luisa**	**Il trovatore**	**La Bohème**	**Tannhäuser**	
Miller	*Levine;*	*Levine;*	**Miller**	*Conlon;*	*Levine;*	*Levine;*	
Santi;	*Kubiak,*	*Stratas,*	*Santi;*	*Price,*	*Stratas,*	*Rysanek,*	
Ricciarelli,	*Dunn,*	*Scotto,*	*Ricciarelli,*	*V. Cortez,*	*Scotto,*	*Cornell,*	
Berini,	*Cassilly,*	*Carreras,*	*Berini,*	*Giacomini,*	*Carreras,*	*Brenneis,*	
Carreras,	*Weikl,*	*Stilwell,*	*Alexander,*	*Quilico*	*Stilwell,*	*Weikl,*	
Nucci,	*Berberian*	*Monk,*	*Nucci,*		*Monk,*	*Macurdy*	
Plishka		*Morris*	*Kavrakos*		*Morris*		

The Media and Publicity

The evening of Monday, January 11 was frozen. A cold front had swept over the entire United States, and in the spaces of Lincoln Center the temperature seemed far colder as the winds whipped around the great plaza, which in summertime is a gathering place for strollers, gawkers, and performance-goers, some lining up at the temporary booth to buy cones filled with New York's excellent Sedutto ice cream.

Approaching the Met, I saw several people holding up tickets for sale: strange in the cold, and stranger because Luciano Pavarotti was singing (the opera, incidentally, was Verdi's *Luisa Miller*). That oddity was cleared up on entering the Met, for a sign proclaimed a change of cast: Pavarotti was indisposed. Those sidewalk entrepreneurs who had bought tickets early and hoped to profit from the appearance of opera's greatest media star had been literally left in the cold. There was, however, a measure of consolation: Pavarotti's cover, the veteran tenor John

Alexander, was similarly indisposed, and the Met had prevailed upon another leading tenor, José Carreras, to step in "at very short notice" (he had sung the role not long before at Covent Garden).

Operagoers are inured to cancellations, which occur throughout the season and now and then reach epidemic proportions. The Met, of course, does not refund money for changes in cast, but only when the opera itself has to be changed (an eventuality it goes to great lengths to prevent). Subscribers and visitors are usually caught short by cancellations, but the opera-buff grapevine is quite accurate in this regard—it often knows before the house does—and any opera buff is aware of the singers who are most likely to cancel (Montserrat Caballé, Teresa Stratas) and those who rarely do (Joan Sutherland, Birgit Nilsson).* The multiple-cover system is designed to act as a safety net and is indispensable for a subscriber repertory house.† It also adds measurably to the cost of opera in New York; singers can often make a decent annual wage without ever setting foot onstage.

Those who saw the notice upon entering accepted it with stoicism, as a standard vicissitude of operatic life ("I've never heard him yet, but that's show biz").

The performance itself, even though it was the first for that revival and thus attended by the major critics, was one of those that define repertory opera at its most routine. While it was not sloppy or offhand, it was the sort of evening when nothing much was out of place, but nothing much *took* place, either on-

---

*There are also singers who, upon reading the reviews of their performances, decide to become suddenly indisposed for the remainder of the run, or at least for the broadcast (which is likely to be taped). The management looks indulgently upon this, if the singer is important enough.

†The management has considerably tightened rules regarding covers in the last few years. Met Assistant Manager Joan Ingpen says that there are two categories, first and second covers. First covers are now guaranteed to go on if the scheduled singer cancels, while with second covers an attempt may be made to find another singer; if that fails, the second cover will perform. Often first covers who stand by loyally are granted a performance or two in the next season.

stage or in the pit. *Luisa Miller* is a difficult opera, for it is overlong and must be handled with loving care to make its dramatic points. The cast was competent but in no way special, and Katia Ricciarelli in the title role demonstrated that on that night her voice was at some distance from its best. Her approximations of pitch, allied to a resolutely complacent stage deportment, only dragged out the proceedings, further attenuated by the deliberate pacings of that singer's conductor Nello Santi, who for some reason had been re-engaged by the company. (Someone remarked, rightly, "His fast tempi have neither weight nor propulsion, and his slow tempi have neither fluidity nor grace.") Only Carreras's vitality of voice—though often pushed to its limit—kept the evening alive (he also looked the part, even if, understandably, he often did not know quite where to move next).

It is this type of performance, more than the demonstrably slipshod or disastrous one, that is the bane of repertory (as opposed to festival) opera. It is opera squeezed from a toothpaste tube, and far blander than toothpaste.

And yet it is precisely this type of performance that is put forward by those in the opera house as exemplifying the merit of the Met. "Night after night," they insist, "the level of performance at the Met is higher than in any other repertory house in the world, but this is never mentioned in the press."

The statement is probably true, although today there are few opera houses that perform on such a continuous basis. Certainly this *Luisa Miller* was on a higher level of accomplishment than, as some horror stories have it, an off night at the Vienna Staatsoper, for instance. But this only spotlights the underlying problem of repertory opera: that an adequate evening's performance, while maintaining a certain level and not actively driving away the subscribers (who may be bored, but feel it is simply their reaction, not the fault of the company), may be wholly inadequate as a homage to that opera and to that composer. This is not trivial. If every performance is, as it should ideally be, in some sense sacramental, then such an evening, despite its consistency, has failed. Verdi has only been nodded at, not served. It is the task of those outside the house—outside the daily concerns of the repertory—to point it out. And this means the press.

Publicity is the lifeblood of any performing organization, and it comes from three sources. One kind of publicity is sent out by the organization itself; another is spread through word of mouth; and the third is disseminated by the press and allied media through reviews, news items, interviews, and feature pieces. The Met's press office, headed by David Reuben, takes care of the press in terms of tickets, arrangements for interviews and photographs, and any information about the Met and its activities. A representative of the press office is in the house until the final curtain to explain any changes of cast or to answer questions about the cuts or whether the soprano transposed her big aria. (Critics often think they know, not always correctly; prudence dictates a simple question to the press office. This year, for example, only one tenor sang "Di quella pira" in *Il trovatore* at its correct pitch.)

The Met, of course, because of its international renown, generates its own publicity independent of any agency. And for many years that publicity was centered on the figure of Francis Robinson ("Mr. Met"), whose portrait now graces the press room, and to whose memory the Saturday-matinee Verdi Requiem was dedicated. It is no exaggeration to say that outside New York, Robinson exemplified the Met more than did any general manager; and even within the city, his visibility and his endless fund of stories about the company (often involving his beloved Enrico Caruso) made him better known than even Rudolf Bing. He was the quintessential after-dinner speaker, full of appropriate quotes, and ever optimistic about the future of the Met. He could make you believe that the worst singer was worthy of being heard, as long as he or she was on the Met roster; and he turned aside difficult questions with charm, a smile, and another story. His knowledge of the Met was so extensive (if selective) that he seemed a walking repository of the company's history.

The situation with the Met and the press is quite different from that involving the New York theater or the movies. First of all, the aim is different. With a play or a film, good publicity leads to ticket sales and an extended, and profitable, run. At the Met, the run is predetermined, and mostly already sold. Good reviews may ensure the return of the opera in future seasons, although by the time of those reviews the revival has already been scheduled. And by the time of the revival, the work's novelty may have worn off; it is a given that the public would rather go to a fresh hit than to a rerun—and will pay extra to do so. The Met found itself with an unsuspected hit in 1981's *Parade* triple bill—it was not scheduled for the current season—and is hoping that the memory will hold until the production is revived in 1982–83.

For the central core operas, however, reviews have but minimal effect, though in the longer run a consistency of negative reviews will begin to take its toll.

The music critic differs from the theater or film critic in that what he reviews either is part of history at the time of the review's appearance or will shortly be history, for that season at least. There were, for instance, eight performances of the Stravinsky triple bill, the first on December 4 and the last on January 2. While a "selling" review will affect ticket sales, it must appear quite soon to be effective. This means that the music critic is, to an extent, freed from the burden of feeling that he has an economic as well as an artistic impact upon the performance. Yet often his impact is strong: the negative tone of John Rockwell's review of *La Bohème* in *The New York Times* came as a shock to those behind stage, who felt they had a blockbuster hit as well as a blockbuster production, and for a few days morale was distinctly lower.

Another important difference between the opera critic and the others (including popular-music critics) is that the latter deal largely, if not exclusively, with the new, while the former reviews a repertory consisting basically of the old, which many of them have seen dozens of times. This situation necessarily imposes a separate set of criteria and breeds a group who prefer to live in the past than in the present.

There are only three daily mass-circulation newspapers left in

New York City, and of these only *The New York Times* carries any substantial musical-critical weight. It is in fact a critical monopoly. Both the *Post* and the *News* have cut back coverage of classical music, and each review they carry has likewise been pared to the minimum.*

Yet if the *Times* has a monopoly, it is hardly the only critical voice. Indeed, among the opera buffs who deign to read the press, the reviews in the *Times* count for less than reviews elsewhere.

The most important of these other voices is undoubtedly Andrew Porter in *The New Yorker*, which publishes his reviews with about a ten-day to two-week delay. Porter is known for his expertise in the field of opera, and if some consider his essays too historical and "musicological," they are both comprehensive and cogent, and provide a counterweight to the necessary shorthand of the "overnight" review (as do the often subsequent Sunday pieces in the *Times*). Peter G. Davis, an ex-*Times* critic newly installed at *New York* magazine, is another critic with a wide knowledge of opera and singing and a commensurate enthusiasm. Leighton Kerner, the indefatigable performance trotter writing for *The Village Voice*, writes a column that has the merit of manifold attendance at performances, scholarship, and boundless zest for music of all sorts. The dean of New York music critics, Irving Kolodin (who is the unofficial Met historian by virtue of his book on the company's history), wrote a music column in the *Saturday Review* for decades, and latterly he has written for Long Island's *Newsday*.

The press department, however, deals with many more critics than these. Indeed, because of the Met's international renown, it is in the position of having to dole out its few press tickets to a great number of claimants. (In addition, on occasions such as the Stravinsky triple bill, it has to accommodate the dance and art press as well.) These include second critics on newspapers (the *Times* in particular, which reviews major cast changes) and critics

---

*The *News*'s music critic, William Zakariasen, has the distinction of having been on the Met's roster for several years in comprimario parts, including Harry in *La fanciulla del West* and Leopold in *Der Rosenkavalier*.

for other, smaller newspapers and magazines in the city, such as the vital ethnic press: Italian (*Il Progresso*), German (*Aufbau, Staatszeitung*), black (Raoul Abdul in the *Amsterdam News*), French (*France-Amérique*), and Spanish (*Temas*). The last three are more likely to review performances when blacks or French- or Spanish-speaking artists are in the cast. The Associated Press, UPI, *Time*, and *Newsweek* also cover major events. And the growth of the suburbs as well as of a national chain press has been reflected by both local, ex-urban coverage and coverage on a regular basis from the Gannett and Newhouse chains to papers around the country.

But the Met's servicing of the press does not end with the greater New York area. Critics from around the country and from Canada visit during the year, particularly from Met tour cities, as do critics from around the world. Such foreign papers as England's *Times, Financial Times*, and *Guardian*, Germany's *Frankfurter Allgemeine*, and Puerto Rico's *Il Diario* run coverage, and the press office has dealt with critics from the likely countries of England, France, Germany, and Italy as well as the less likely ones of Australia, Finland, Japan, and several in South America. If tickets are available, the press office often provides them to feature writers or interviewers, for today's publicity comes as much from personality pieces as from straight criticism. It also sells tickets to those in the field who are not writing on the Met. Television has shown little interest in opera except for an Occasion, but on a "media night" (or if the President decides to show up) it will inundate the premises with overkill.

"The juggling of tickets so that no one feels left out is the single biggest headache we have," said Johanna Fiedler, the Met's press representative. "We simply don't have enough press tickets to go around."

Other headaches come from artists who don't want to be interviewed, for whatever reasons. Some younger artists, for instance, intensely dislike the sort of prying into personal life that is endemic to today's interviews—the so-called *People* magazine approach. They would rather not be interviewed than subject themselves to beside-the-artistic-point articles. Since most professional interviewers (as opposed to music critics who do interviews) are only foggily aware of the specifics of opera—and in any case write for editors and a public uninterested in stagione, *Fach*, transpositions, or artistic goals—the talk will naturally turn to questions of whether sex before singing is a good thing, or what happened when the tenor fell down the flight of steps onstage. (The ancillary, but germane, question of the effect of the menstrual cycle on a singer's performance is, however, rarely discussed.)

Since the job of the press department is to publicize, it is unhappy when artists do not cooperate. John Dexter's notorious hatred of the press has prevented preproduction publicity for several of his directorial ventures. This year, for example, the Met was anxious to get prepublicity for the Stravinsky evening, an iffy ticket proposition, and was encouraged to learn that John Russell (who has since become the *New York Times*'s chief art critic) would write a *Times Magazine* piece on the event for publication on the Sunday previous to the premiere, with lots of color sketches of David Hockney's sets and costumes. But Hockney refused to allow any advance publication of his ideas, and the *Times* felt that unless the material could be run before the premiere, it would not be newsworthy; the Sunday after would not do. Thus, the piece was never written.

Finally, there are a very few critics who refuse to take free press tickets and insist on buying (or having their publication buy) whatever tickets they want. Samuel Lipman is one of these: he feels freer to express his opinions on the Met when he is not, as it were, a guest.

This brings up an underlying aspect of the critic's relationship to a performing organization, especially one as pervasive and powerful as the Met—an aspect that has relatively little to do with whether the critic is right or wrong about a specific point (always the bane of the press office). That is: To what extent is the critic serving the organization as an unpaid flack? This leads to the excusing of faults that should be censured, just as the opposite tack leads to unjustified charges masquerading as critical freedom.

Each working critic must answer that question for himself or herself.

The great majority of critics covering the Met on a regular basis are in sympathy with the general aims of that repertory company. They are for the most part as conservatively oriented as the management and have little use for "modern opera" or for the radical developments in opera production from abroad. Those critics who are not in sympathy either stay away entirely or fulminate at odd intervals. (The leading current Jacobin is the aptly named Kenneth Furie, who attacks the Met from his monthly column for *Keynote*, the magazine of New York classical music station WNCN.)

Overall, the general media, with its attitude of news first, analysis second, and, all too often, understanding last, will highlight the Met only when it is a matter of a public personality fight, an operatic brouhaha onstage, or a fiscal or labor crisis. Probing questions at Met press conferences are seldom heard. It is usually the time-honored parade of subjects (Why isn't X singer or Y conductor at the Met? Why are Z singer and A conductor at the Met? Why is B opera performed and C opera not?), while the management goes blithely on its way.

J	A	N	U	A	R	Y	
18	19	20	21	22	23	23	
Il trovatore	**La Bohème**	**Luisa**	**Tannhäuser**	**La Bohème**	**Luisa**	**Il trovatore**
Conlon;	*Levine;*	**Miller**	*Levine;*	*Levine;*	**Miller**	*Conlon;*
Price,	*Zoghby,*	*Santi;*	*Rysanek,*	*Stratas,*	*Santi;*	*Price,*
V. Cortez,	*Scotto,*	*Ricciarelli,*	*Cornell,*	*Migenes-*	*Ricciarelli,*	*V. Cortez,*
Giacomini,	*Carreras,*	*Berini,*	*Brenneis,*	*Johnson,*	*Berini,*	*Giacomini,*
Quilico	*Edwards,*	*Pavarotti,*	*Weikl,*	*Carreras,*	*Pavarotti,*	*Quilico*
	Monk,	*Nucci,*	*Macurdy*	*Stilwell,*	*Nucci,*	
	Robbins	*Plishka*		*Monk,*	*Plishka*	
				Robbins		

The Monument

M onday, January 18 was another frigid evening; when traffic was light, the front-door ushers huddled next to an electric heater that glowed incongruously on the marble floor. A wave of the annual cold-and-flu bug had swept the house, backstage and front, and discreet sniffling could be heard.

Inside, the bill of fare was the second performance of Verdi's *Il trovatore*. The Leonora was Leontyne Price.

Leonora had been Price's debut role in the opera house, and has always been one of her most famous. The lovely last-act aria "D'amor sull'ali rosee" seemed created by Verdi especially for Price's voice, showing off the legato and the creaminess of tone for which she is famous.

When the lights went up on the second scene of the first act, Price could be seen upstage, her back to the audience. Very slowly, she turned for her opening measures. I was reminded then, as I am often reminded when seeing Price nowadays, of the final scene in Virgil Thomson's *The Mother of Us All*, where Susan B. (Anthony) is enshrined onstage as a monument, which comes to life to sing the glorious closing pages Thomson wrote for her. (It is a pity that no impresario had the wit to cast Price in this role, for she would have been magnificent.) Price is now a monument, and, curiously enough, her voice has become one with her persona.

Once Price's voice was freely produced, but after some vocal difficulties a few years back—not unknown in the mid-careers of singers—it emerged as a simulacrum of what it had been before, but now subject to iron control. Each note she produces seems willed into existence from her throat, each phrase exactly calculated; in contrast, fast passages and portamento tend to perilousness simply because they cannot be subject to that same control. I cannot imagine Price any longer giving herself utterly to a role, in the way that Leonie Rysanek and Teresa Stratas give themselves. Price has become, in both voice and deportment, the stereotypical Prima Donna, moving as imperturbably through the proceedings onstage as the *Queen Mary* used to move up the Hudson among the tugs to her dock.

This attitude carries with it a great deal of authority. It should, for Leontyne Price knows that she stands not only for an operatic soprano but for a wider constituency, the black singer. Price onstage consciously assumes black aspirations and black achievement in opera, and she is fully aware of her regal position. And blacks come to her performances as to a state occasion.

Opera has been—certainly since the overpublicized debut of Marian Anderson at the Met focused attention on the black singer, but even prior to that—a route of upward mobility for young blacks. Blacks feel that this situation is much better for the female singer than for the male (bass-baritone Simon Estes, who made his debut at the Met in a repertory opera during the 1981–82 season—he had sung in a concert performance earlier—is outspoken on this subject). At the Met, there are a number of younger black singers on the roster, and tenor Philip Creech, mezzo Isola Jones, and soprano Kathleen Battle have been extensively showcased by the management, both in the house and in James Levine's Music from Ravinia series in Alice Tully Hall.

Black singers by and large look to Leontyne Price rather than to other leading black singers—Jessye Norman, Shirley Verrett, or Grace Bumbry—as their spiritual leader, because she was earlier in the field, has maintained her eminence over a span of years and numerous recordings (including many recital discs), and has planned her career not as a *prima donna d'opera* but as a *black* prima donna. Other black singers have concentrated on European careers, but Price remains tied to this country. She has always been in the forefront of civil rights activities, has appeared many times before congressional committees, and has kept in the spotlight as a spokeswoman and a figurehead.

This rise to prominence of the black singer has itself raised an issue in opera (no less than on the spoken stage) that has been too little discussed in the media—that is, the extent to which the pride of an underclass should control the demands of an artistic work. Specifically, the question is not whether a black singer should be barred from playing white roles—an emphatically racist position— but whether a black should wear whiteface to sing Violetta or Norma. It is generally accepted that in these kinds of roles a black singer should not be required to look white. But certain operatic roles demand "whiteness" in their essence: for example, Elsa in *Lohengrin* and Pamina in *Die Zauberflöte*. The contrast of white and dark is explicitly demanded by Wagner in *Lohengrin,* while Schikaneder and Mozart also specifically contrasted the "evil" of the blackamoor Monostatos with the white skin of Pamina. (Today, opera directors tend to make Monostatos into a buffoonish caricature and/or to costume him in some outlandish way, in order to avoid the evil black–good white implication, though when Monostatos attempts to steal a kiss—at the least—from the sleeping Pamina, Sarastro castigates him with the explicit words, "Your soul is as black as your face.") Should Martina Arroyo have sung Elsa, and Kathleen Battle Pamina, as both have done at the Met, without making themselves up as white women? To blacks, whiteface remains unacceptable. Critics such as John Simon maintain that unless blacks are willing to transform themselves, as any white singer or actor would to play Otello or Othello, they should be denied the parts, and that this decision has nothing to do with racism. Other critics, such as Charles Shere of the Oakland *Tribune,* argue that the overriding social climate of the times necessitates a compromise. Until black singers can feel comfortable enough in the society to be able to put on whiteface without feeling degraded by it, such a decision should not be demanded of them, even if the artistic result is affected.

Whatever the merits of that issue, the fact is that Leontyne Price has become today less a singer performing whatever role she undertakes than a symbol who consents to grace the stage. In the past, Mattia Battistini refused to play roles beneath his dignity as a star; the same can be said of Price. (I cannot imagine her, even if her voice were right for the part, playing the maid Despina in *Così fan tutte,* as Kathleen Battle did. There are simply too many overtones of the sassy Negro servant of 1930s plays and movies that inhere to the role, even if it is entirely within the Italian commedia dell'arte tradition.)

Certainly this condign majesty suffuses every performance she gives. Price was never an accomplished actress, although in her earlier days she managed a kind of feminine vulnerability that accorded with roles such as Aida. But now, whatever acting takes place is sculptured—the hands raised in supplication, the head ever held high—and this restrained nobility coincides with the regulated flow of notes from her throat. It is not surprising that Price is better in arias than in ensembles, for she represents the kind of aria-only singing typified in opera seria, whose heroines were similarly outsized and distant in terms of their emotions. Around her the rest of the cast, which included such Verdians as Louis Quilico and Giuseppe Giacomini, were reduced to pygmies. She dominated the evening, to the delight of her supporters.

Price's career, no less than her resolute surmounting of the vocal troubles she encountered, is a tribute to her hard work and her unwavering sense of self. Whenever she appears—and those moments are carefully chosen—she carries with her the aura of an old-fashioned prima donna. But she carries more than that. She stands for her people, and neither we nor she is ever allowed to forget it.

In a musical genre that dotes on prima donnas of both sexes, Leontyne Price is the genuine article.

J A N U A R Y

25	26	27	28	29	30	30
Tannhäuser	**Luisa**	**La Bohème**	**Il trovatore**	**Così fan**	**Tannhäuser**	**Luisa**
Levine;	**Miller**	*Levine;*	*Conlon;*	**tutte**	*Levine;*	**Miller**
Rysanek,	*Santi;*	*Stratas,*	*Price,*	*Levine;*	*Rysanek,*	*Santi;*
Dunn,	*Maliponte,*	*Migenes-*	*V. Cortez,*	*Te Kanawa,*	*Dunn,*	*Maliponte,*
Cassilly,	*Berini,*	*Johnson,*	*Mauro,*	*Battle,*	*Cassilly,*	*Berini,*
Monk,	*Pavarotti,*	*Carreras,*	*Quilico*	*Ewing,*	*Weikl,*	*Pavarotti,*
Macurdy	*Nucci,*	*Stilwell,*		*Rendall,*	*Macurdy*	*Sereni,*
	Plishka	*Monk,*		*Morris,*		*Plishka*
		Robbins		*Gramm*		

"Così fan tutte" and the Big House

M ozart's opera *Così fan tutte* (1790) is an intimate work, which has been called a sextet for voices. It is written for three men and three women, a small chorus, and the orchestra of Mozart's time. Yet, despite its intimacy, it has achieved almost eighty performances at the Met, and its previous production, in 1951, was both a critical and a popular success—it even resulted in a recording. Was this success because it was Mozart, who becomes with each passing year ever more immune from all criticism? Or was it his music for this particular opera, an endlessly exfoliated succession of melody? Or was it that *Così* places the direct focus on voice, and not on spectacle, acting, or even plot? Doubtless it is a combination of the three. *Così*, however, remains an intimate opera. Should it, then, have a place in the Met's repertory, since the Met is a thirty-eight-hundred-seat house in which intimacy is alien?

The question raised by *Così* is not a frivolous one. A given at the

Met is that as an opera house, it is best adapted to large-scale works. Anything smaller than the nineteenth-century operas of the repertory will immediately lose that sense of contact vital for ideal appreciation. If James Levine feels that Stravinsky's *The Rake's Progress*, an opera with a full singing complement and a full chorus, is too small for the Met, what is *Così* doing there?

The idea that a top-level repertory opera company should have not one but two houses, one large and one small, has particular application in the United States, for most of this country's opera houses are, by European standards, grossly outsized. London's Covent Garden, Milan's La Scala, Vienna's Staatsoper, and even Paris's Opéra are all much smaller venues, and the Milan company boasts a second house, the Piccola Scala, in which it can play the smaller-scale works. First-time visitors from Europe to the Met are invariably awed by the size of the auditorium and cannot imagine how opera can effectively be sung there.

And yet it is, because of the acoustics and because the company generally chooses the type of voices that will show to advantage in its environs.*

If, to the idealist, the Met is off-limits to operas like *Così*, to others that question is not so easily answered. Levine, in an interview in *The New York Times* on January 17, 1982, tentatively suggested the possibility of the Met's expanding into an additional, smaller house (an idea he believes in strongly), although the technical and financial problems attached to that decision have engendered skepticism on the board level. Doubtless it would be better to hear *Così* in a theater the size of Glyndebourne (and to hear *La Bohème* there as well), but it is increasingly evident that this is, alas, only an ideal.

All major operas, and quite a few others, share a quality that is

---

*The management is, in fact, sometimes overly cautious in this respect. Elisabeth Söderström is rightly termed, in *The Concise Oxford Dictionary of Opera*, "one of the finest singing actresses of the 1960s and 1970s," and she sang to splendid effect in the old house for several seasons. Yet when I spoke to her good friend and countryman Goeran Gentele, he maintained flatly that the Lincoln Center house was too big for her voice. She has not yet sung there, though she is scheduled for the future.

inbuilt in any effective stagework: the flexibility of their emotional appeal. One can be persuaded by a *Così* at the Met if it is performed well, just as one can be persuaded by small-scale operas of lesser stature, such as Poulenc's *Les Mamelles de Tirésias.* The New York City Opera, in the acoustically less forgiving spaces of the New York State Theater, even achieved success with Poulenc's monodrama *La Voix humaine,* by definition an intimate work (one soprano, one bed, one telephone).

The argument in favor of a smaller house for smaller-scale works, then, is one of intimacy of feeling, in part as relates to the voices but specifically, in terms of the Met, as relates to the size of the auditorium. Just as hearing a string quartet in a medium-size drawing room, where one can feel the vibrations of the music through the soles of one's feet as well as in one's ears, is preferable to hearing the same quartet in a small concert hall (I leave aside the lunacy of listening to a quartet, as frequently happens, in Carnegie Hall), so hearing opera in a venue like the Juilliard Theater adds much to its attractiveness, both in terms of a more active participation in the events onstage and in terms of being able to hear not the notes, but the words—important in operas with recitative or operas in English.

The Met and other large houses cannot afford that luxury, and if the Met is to present the core repertory, which includes small-scale works, it must adjust both its approach and the works' essence to achieve an effective result.

This means, in the case of *Così,* a tailoring of the visual and an attention to the auditory. The size of the Met's stage must be reduced and disguised, through the creation of a false proscenium with its own curtain, thus channeling attention to a smaller playing area. (In fact, of course, as any standee knows, only a relatively small part of the Met's large stage is ever used for solo singing. John Dexter's stagings over and over pushed the singers toward the front of the stage and kept them there, so that they could better project their voices into the auditorium. This was quite consistent with the bad old days of opera directing.)

Voices of Met size should be employed. This is tricky in Mozart, whose music demands a flexibility and a lightness of legato more attuned to younger voices; in Mozart, a heavy, thickly moving voice is unpleasantly evident in a way it is not in Verdi, Puccini, or Wagner. When the Met produced Così in 1951, two of the singers—Eleanor Steber and Richard Tucker—had big voices, and in subsequent revivals such singers as Leontyne Price were used.

The casting of this Così was likewise selected with attention to size as well as Mozartean Fach. Kiri Te Kanawa is certainly among today's greatest Mozart singers, but her voice also has a heft and tone that can fill the Met. James Morris, as Guglielmo, also has a large, somewhat rough voice, as befits someone whose repertory includes Don Giovanni, Billy Budd's evil Claggart, and Boris Godunov. Despite its size, though, he retains the ability to sing softly well, thus not unbalancing the ensembles.

And this is the key. Mozart requires, in all of his core repertory operas with the possible exception of Die Zauberflöte, an ensemble cohesiveness and unity (arguably at its most concentrated in Così) that are central to his music making. If one voice dominates or (more crucially) does not blend with the others, that ensemble will disintegrate. The consequent loss will be greater than, say, in Verdi, for Mozart's ensembles are written from the viewpoint of chamber music, not of voices in full cry. Today, Mozartean ensemble singing is on a higher level of ease and ingrained knowledge than it was at the end of the Second World War, and can almost be taken as a given rather than as something that has to be painstakingly taught to a cast in rehearsal. The effect of such singing is to enlarge the sound and to make it more dominating, and thus to an extent vitiate the constraints built into Così.

The finish and polish of the whole were, indeed, quite winning, so that even lighter voices, such as David Rendall's as Ferrando, gained from their surroundings. (What should also be remembered—it is quite often forgotten by impresarios no less than by opera buffs—is that the size of a voice is less an issue than its projection. Huge, diffused voices may stop at the footlights, while smaller, focused ones may thrill the back rows.) Likewise, the soft playing of the orchestra, and the soft singing of the soloists, did

not work against communication; in fact, they enhanced it, because the variations of dynamics produced varieties of tension-
and-release and shadings of color that kept the audience's attention. Ideally, perhaps, *Così* and such works as Ravel's *L'Enfant et les
sortilèges* should be performed elsewhere, but the compromises
that have to be taken into account when those operas are done at
the Met are not, finally, self-defeating.

Levine very much wants to establish a Mozart tradition at the
Met, to go along with the Verdi and Wagner traditions; and to that
end he has scheduled productions of all of Mozart's major operas.
The aim is neither quixotic nor chimeric.

			F E B R U A R Y			
1	*2*	*3*	*4*	*5*	*6*	*6*
La Bohème	**Il trovatore**	**Così fan tutte**	**Tannhäuser**	**La Bohème**	**Il trovatore**	**Così fan tutte**
Levine;	*Conlon;*	*Levine;*	*Levine;*	*Levine;*	*Conlon;*	*Levine;*
Zylis-Gara,	*Price,*	*Te Kanawa,*	*Rysanek,*	*Zylis-Gara,*	*Price,*	*Te Kanawa,*
Migenes-	*V. Cortez,*	*Battle,*	*Dunn,*	*Craig,*	*V. Cortez,*	*Battle,*
Johnson,	*Giacomini,*	*Ewing,*	*Cassilly,*	*Ciannella,*	*Giacomini,*	*Ewing,*
Ciannella,	*Quilico*	*Rendall,*	*Weikl,*	*Ellis,*	*Quilico*	*Rendall,*
Ellis,		*Morris,*	*Macurdy*	*Monk,*		*Morris,*
Monk,		*Gramm*		*Robbins*		*Gramm*
Robbins						

The Fly in Amber

The Metropolitan Opera Saturday-afternoon broadcast (there are twenty this season) is one of the longest-running continuous radio shows and long predates the sponsorship of Texaco. Apart from the tours, it was the Met's original outreach effort, and it remains a cornerstone of the Met's attitude that it is a national opera company. *Opera News* has in recent years gotten away from a weekly publication schedule hitched to the broadcasts, but each winter issue focuses on them, with casts, articles, and interviews with the singers.

The pressures to sing on a Saturday broadcast are appreciable. Stars are more likely to be scheduled, are more likely to give involved performances, and are less likely to cancel for whimsical reasons. For these reasons the Saturday matinee, which used to be one of the easier tickets to obtain, is now one of the more difficult, and if the proverbial matinee ladies are still in heavy attendance, the audience is generally more responsive and less apt to start the march homeward during the final act.

The broadcasts themselves were for many years produced by the formidable Geraldine Souvaine and featured the mellifluous voice (and, at times, strange pronunciation) of Milton Cross as announcer. Cross died a few years ago, to be succeeded in that position by Peter Allen, and Souvaine retired at the end of the 1980–81 season. Her successor is Richard Mohr, the ex-RCA classical-record producer who was for many years a fixture as a panelist on the broadcasts.

The intermission features of the Saturday-afternoon broadcasts form an integral part of the whole and have, over the years, become as immutable as the operas themselves, to the evident satisfaction of most longtime listeners in the United States and Canada, if to the exasperation of others.

It is a format that could be termed a soothing blend of information and chat, not as bland as video talk shows, but rarely exhibiting any cutting edge. Over the years these features have bred a group of "stars," analogous to the ones onstage but longer-lived, which has included Sigmund Spaeth (the once-famous "tune detective," whose passion for *Die Meistersinger* influenced more than one budding Wagnerian), Deems Taylor, John Coveney, Terry McEwen (now Terence A. McEwen, general director of the San Francisco Opera), and Boris Goldovsky. Edward Downes, son of the late *New York Times* music critic Olin Downes, has succeeded Cross as the best-known Saturday-afternoon radio voice, both as quizmaster of the "Texaco Opera Quiz" and as lecturer and occasional panelist.

There are fewer intermission features nowadays than there were a few decades back because there are fewer intermissions. In the past, one-act operas such as *Salome* and short ones such as *Don Pasquale* and *Hansel and Gretel* were paired with ballets. The shorter length of programs today (seen clearly in symphony concerts) has led the Met to drop second works, thus saving money. Similarly, many operas of four and five acts are now played with only two intermissions instead of three or four, for faster pacing, because audiences want less intermission time (they get home earlier) and— no small consideration—because the staging abilities of the new house, with its opportunities for fully set scenes to be ready in the wings or below (or above) stage and be moved into place in less than a minute, have meant that the time needed for once-cumbersome set changes has been considerably reduced. (Also reduced have been the shouts of stagehands behind the curtain, and the rumbling of the stage trucks, always a distraction.)

The Met can now set up the immensely complicated first- and second-act sets of *La Bohème* so smoothly that it has dispensed with the intermission between the acts, on the rationale that the acts are continuous in time—the bohemians go from their garret directly to the streets of Paris. (The most notorious such change is the playing of *Wozzeck* without intermissions, or the first three acts of Debussy's *Pelléas et Mélisande;* Levine maintains this is done because of the natural curve of the music. Musical fidelity, it seems, does not extend to intermissions.)

Verdi's four-act *Il trovatore,* broadcast on February 6, retained its three intermissions, however (probably because of the monumentality of the ugly sets), and thus made for much activity in the Met's List Hall. List Hall (named for donor Albert A. List, not for basso Emanuel) is a 144-seat enclave to the left of the auditorium, downstairs and past the press office; a bust of Milton Cross stands, like Cerberus, in the foyer. The hall is used mainly for chorus rehearsals, but occasional lectures are given there, and all intermission features. These are open to the public, who must be in their seats within a minute after curtain fall, leading to a stampede of the habitués. (The sessions end four minutes before curtain rise, thus giving the audience more of a chance to get back to their seats.)

Il trovatore has two scenes in the second act, and some people, not realizing this, appeared in List Hall during the pause between scenes. Mohr urbanely greeted them and told them they were welcome to sit for the seventeen-minute second scene, but that it was not yet an intermission; this led to a reverse stampede, for the auditorium closes its doors at the first notes of music, and those outside must wait until the next intermission or watch the show on the television set outside List Hall.

Guild members may listen to the intermissions in the Belmont

Room, where they are broadcast; and not infrequently, when the feature is prerecorded rather than live, List Hall hosts an audience quietly listening to a tape recorder.

But all three February 6 intermissions were live, and two were hoary Met-broadcast standard features. The first was "Opera News on the Air," a discussion of the afternoon's opera with piano examples. Usually this is the province of Boris Goldovsky, but today as a change it was being done by the American playwright and opera buff Terrence McNally.

Timings may be crucial to opera; running past the magic hour of midnight involves extra payment under union contracts *from the starting time.* Rudolf Bing was paranoid about running over (the bon mot was that at one minute to midnight he would jump into the pit and begin conducting furiously), but the current management seems to take a more relaxed attitude, for this year's *Tannhäuser* and *Parsifal* regularly overstepped pumpkin time. But timing is far more crucial to the intermission features, for the music never waits. When I arrived at List Hall at 11:45 a.m., Richard Mohr, stopwatch in hand, accompanist William Vendice, and McNally were running through McNally's already prepared script, timing not only the reading of the text but the length of the musical excerpts. McNally was told by Mohr that he could not talk over the playing of the music, since the two could not be adequately balanced with the equipment they had—"Maybe next year we'll be able to get the kind of equipment to make it possible." After two read-throughs the timing was fixed, only to be changed when, fifteen minutes before the broadcast, it was learned that two and a half minutes would have to be shaved off. Mohr and McNally red-penciled sections of the finished draft, timed the excisions, and trusted to luck.

McNally, in a blue blazer, looked slightly nervous, and was counseled by Mohr not to look at the audience, but to read from his script. (The script itself is submitted about two weeks prior to the broadcast and is then edited by Mohr for length and content.) As the two worked on the cuts, one usher set up the time-honored chimes that signal the end of the opera quiz and practiced on them a motif from the day's opera; the tuner finished putting the piano in optimum order; and usher Stephen Shapiro quietly worked on needlepoint. Mohr's assistant, Vinnie Volpe, set up cards reading "McNally" and "Mohr" for the benefit of the audience. In the background one could hear Peter Allen, from his broadcast booth on the Grand Tier level, introduce the opera, and the performance began. Shortly before the act ended, the radio technician, Ed Beaty, had McNally speak into the microphone to adjust the balance. McNally popped a throat lozenge into his mouth. All was in readiness.

The audience streamed in and was quickly seated ("All the way to the center of the aisles, please") and greeted by Mohr. McNally began to read. The talk was a once-over-lightly on *Il trovatore,* with several short piano examples, from McNally's viewpoint. Thus, the aria "Tacea la notte" "blossoms and opens like the petals of a flower," every note of Manrico's tenor music is "breathtaking," "music that sticks to the ribs," while the evil baritone's great aria "Il balen" is "sexy." Mohr stood by the piano, timing the talk while turning pages for Vendice. The speech ended and was mightily applauded. The audience left quickly, and McNally looked relieved. Edward Downes, sitting in the front row, went up and congratulated him.

The stage was now set up for the second intermission feature, the "Texaco Opera Quiz," another long-running, and even more popular, feature. There were three panelists—all regulars. (Sometimes there are four, but Mohr feels that three is the ideal number, since with four someone gets left out.) The three were airline executive Peter Bonelli, recording executive John Pfeiffer, and vocal coach and accompanist Alberta Masiello. Masiello, a formidable woman given to chain-smoking thin brown cigarettes, has for years been one of the most outspoken and colorful presences on the intermissions features. "I get poison letters like crazy," she said, and made some pungent comments to those in the room about what she had heard of the afternoon's performance.

The format for the quiz has been set into concrete. There is at least one "piano question" involving detection of several operatic excerpts. These had been rehearsed by Vendice in the morning, well before the arrival of the panelists. There is also one "discussion question," which the panelists get to choose beforehand. Usually, they are given two or three choices during the preceding week, and when they arrive they vote for the one most likely to produce a lively discussion. After going over the three choices, it was decided that the topic should be whether opera should be sung in the original language or in English—a subject used countless times before, but one that seems to have an inexhaustible hold on the public.

The audience—larger this time, for the quiz is a star turn—streamed in once more, and Edward Downes began his polished introductions. Masiello was most at ease, Bonelli relaxed, and only Pfeiffer exhibited signs of not being used to stage appearances, despite his previous practice. All the panelists agreed that, with minor exceptions, opera should be done in the original language, which found favor with the audience. Verdi's preference for *Otello* in French in Paris, brought up by the wily Downes, was quickly shot down ("He was only being polite"—to which Downes responded that Verdi at that stage of his life did not need to be polite, especially toward an opera house for which he hadn't much affection). Also mentioned was the negative example of the Met's English-language *Bohème* (a frequent citation). The motif from *Trovatore* ended the quiz; as the audience left, one man stayed behind to talk to Downes, telling him that it was his first time at the Met and that he had long wanted to see an opera quiz, which he had heard so many times on the radio.

The final intermission was to be devoted to a "Singers' Round-Table Discussion." This feature is a relative newcomer in popularity, after its introduction some years ago with uninhibited comments from such luminaries as Nilsson, Sutherland, and Horne. But there was some last-minute anxiety, for news had been brought to Vinnie Volpe that one of the panelists, soprano Julia Migenes-Johnson, had discovered on arriving at the stage door that she had lost her wallet outside the restaurant where she had eaten lunch and had gone back to try and find it. Masiello agreed to stay behind to fill in if Migenes-Johnson did not appear. The other two panelists, soprano Gilda Cruz-Romo and mezzo Mignon Dunn, discussed with Mohr their general responses to the question "Have you ever been late to a performance?" and the examples they would use to demonstrate such technical terms as "portamento," "coloring," and "falsetto." Vinnie Volpe set up the cards, leaving out Migenes-Johnson's, and kept a nervous eye on the entrance. Just in time, the singer arrived (without wallet), and Masiello packed up her cigarettes and left, waving goodbye to all, as Migenes-Johnson was given a quick briefing.

The singers were well chosen (though they were not the ones originally listed in *Opera News*), for all of them were voluble, each in a different way. Cruz-Romo spoke with quiet and easy assurance, while Dunn's exuberance—particularly in her telling of how she had arrived at a performance in a hearse, "but not in the back!"—garnered laughs from the audience. Migenes-Johnson, last year's telecast Lulu, looked more like a pop singer of the Barbra Streisand type than an opera soprano, pencil slim in black leather pants and a bouffant hairdo, and her comments were direct and uninhibited. I felt I was seeing a reasonable cross-section of today's opera singers, from the traditional to the new wave, and none of them seemed to be constrained into playing the cliché role of "opera singer" toward the public.* This final intermission feature received the longest applause of the afternoon. After the audience departed, Dunn and Cruz-Romo asked Migenes-Johnson if she needed a lift home, but she told them her husband was on the way to pick her up.

Mohr, in conversation later, said that though he is planning some changes in format for future years, he feels the intermission features are still viable in their present configuration. He prefers live features to prerecorded ones, unless he has no choice, and is

---

*Lincoln Center's "Meet the Artist" program, for groups of twenty or more, has been set up to provide opportunities for informal discussions with singers at the Met or the New York City Opera in which the artist can be seen as a person and not as a character in opera.

trying to schedule enough in advance to meet the deadlines imposed by *Opera News*. Over the years the Texaco intermission features have remained more constant than any other single aspect of the Met's endeavors, and they provide the direct link not only to the five million who listen each week (by the Met's estimate), but to the past. They are flies in amber, and as such are cherished by those who want their nostalgia to be continuous.

			F E B R U A R Y			
8	9	10	11	12	13	13
Norma	**Così fan**	**La Bohème**	**Il trovatore**	**Così fan**	**Norma**	**La Bohème**
Levine;	tutte	Tate;	Conlon;	tutte	Levine;	Tate;
Scotto,	Levine;	Zylis-Gara,	Price,	Levine;	Negri,	Zylis-Gara,
Troyanos,	Te Kanawa,	Craig,	V. Cortez,	Te Kanawa,	Troyanos,	Craig,
Domingo,	Battle,	Ciannella,	Mauro,	Battle,	Domingo,	Ciannella,
Cheek	Ewing,	Ellis,	Quilico	Ewing,	Cheek	Ellis,
	Rendall,	Monk,		Rendall,		Monk,
	Morris,	Robbins		Morris,		Robbins
	Gramm			Gramm		

The Chorus

T he chorus is another integral part of operatic production, and another one that is all too seldom discussed. It appeared, to a greater or lesser extent, in all the operas presented during the week. When it is mentioned, it is usually in negative terms, for the demands on a chorus in a repertory house lead quickly to routine in performance. Added to that, most house choruses are made up of longtime members whose voices, though they may display a maturity not found in "festival choruses," likewise do not have the élan found in younger singers.

Choruses are part of most operas, and an important part of many. Rare is the opera (*Ariadne auf Naxos, Rheingold, Siegfried*) without chorus; and even operas that have reduced choruses, such as *Così fan tutte*, are often trickier to perform than their music would suggest.

David Stivender, who has been the Met's chorus master for eight years, knows thoroughly the problems of managing a repertory opera-house chorus, and it is agreed that he has brought the Met chorus to a high pitch of general efficiency—which does not mean that, on a given night, the results will necessarily be satisfactory. A talk with him is an eye opener, even to a seasoned operagoer, for the vantage point from the chorus gives another perspective entirely.

First of all, the hardest operas for a chorus are not the big choral operas. Stivender maintains that the hardest operas by far are the Italian operas, simply because the chorus in many of them remains in the background.

"So much of it is decorative music, broken up into single syllables which have no meaning, so that each separate entrance is difficult. It is very hard for a chorus to learn and to perform, and the conductor or the prompter cannot be of much help. Bellini's *La sonnambula* is the most difficult opera to teach a chorus."

Stivender sees his task as primarily that of a pedagogue. "It is vitally important to teach the chorus correctly from the first—if I can do that, the opera will stay with them. I begin the task of memorizing from the first rehearsal." This memorization proceeds, first of all, from the articulation of the words rather than from the learning of the music. Stivender maintains that the words, correctly pronounced and enunciated, produce the forward motion that is then encased in the music.

The management has in recent years shown a greater awareness of the problems of choral preparation and scheduling over a thirty-week season, although Stivender (no less than others in the house) complains of lack of rehearsal time.

"This season was a little different—not because of the strike, but because originally, many years ago, when this season was planned, the slot now occupied by the Stravinsky was allotted to [Schoenberg's] *Moses und Aron*. Since *Moses und Aron* is an extremely demanding choral opera, in an unfamiliar style, the schedule was kept light on other chorus operas around that time so as to allow for rehearsal time. *Moses* was postponed, which meant that this fall we had time to work on *Oedipus Rex*, and I was even able to schedule a session to review *Vespri siciliani*, which was coming up in the spring but which we hadn't done for nine years. And when *Frau* was substituted for *Götterdämmerung*, that gave us a bit more time."

Stivender plans his year-long schedule with minute rigorousness, since he has little leeway. The contract settled on after last year's lockout reduced the number of each chorus member's appearances from five to four a week (if a chorus member is scheduled for another, the pay is increased), which meant that scheduling had to be even more carefully planned.

"In operas with small choruses we have to pick the singers, because I don't want any changes during the run of that opera. *Barbiere* this year, for instance, with its revolving stage, is very tricky. You have to be exactly in the right place at the right time."

The stage director can be the bane of the chorus director, for it is he who moves the people around onstage. If a stage director refuses to take account of the chorus's singing problems, the result will be clearly heard—and the chorus will be blamed.

"If you have a director who cannot adapt to the demands, you have problems. Dexter is excellent at working with, rather than against, the chorus, and though I had differences with Otto Schenk when he staged *Tannhäuser*, we were able to work them out to both our satisfactions, and we are currently having no difficulties with his staging of *Les Contes d'Hoffmann*.

"I would prefer to have the chorus downstage, where they can be heard or can easily see the conductor. The difficult part is when a chorus has to come onstage a few at a time and then move about individually, as in *Peter Grimes*."

Offstage singing has always been an especially thorny problem, involving volume, balance, and intelligibility. Stivender says that if the chorus is properly trained, offstage singing should not be difficult, and that the real pitfalls come because the complexity of some of the sets (notably *La Bohème*) mean that they are stored in the wings, waiting to go onstage, and thus severely restrict the offstage areas in which a chorus can stand. "Sometimes we're really squeezed into a shoebox back there."

Such notorious choral moments as the first-act entrance of Butterfly with her female retinue and the first-act wedding chorus of *Le nozze di Figaro* give all chorus directors gray hairs.

"I'd much rather do *Boris Godunov*, which is known as a chorus opera but which doesn't have, really, that much choral music in it, and which is much easier to teach."

What Stivender looks for from his chorus is a combination of color, character, and energy—qualities hard to keep fresh on a night-to-night basis over a season.

"In February, the morale is at its lowest. The tour—which is fun at least for the first few weeks—is far off, Christmas is past, and the season seems endless. New productions keep up the spirit."

Stivender has to be constantly ready for emergencies, which usually mean a reduction of his rehearsal time because of last-minute demands from a stage director; but he was pleased that because some time had somehow been saved, he was able to squeeze in an additional three-hour rehearsal for *Vespri*.

"That gives us enough—with that extra rehearsal we can really put it together."

Although Stivender grumbles about seeing the same faces week after week ("At least conductors get to look at different orchestras now and then!"), he is extremely proud of the accomplishments of his singers.

These singers do not vary much from year to year. (Regular operagoers, with binoculars, like to spot certain choristers in their different wigs, beards, and costumes.)

"Last year we had one opening in the chorus, and this year we'll have none. You can't imagine the number of singers who tried out for that one place!"

Stivender maintains that although he has the unenviable job of weeding out choristers no longer up to vocal standard, he has managed it without undue difficulty.

Aging and routine are the twin burdens on any repertory opera chorus (although New Critics might mention a general lack of acting refinement, and often a visual unsuitability). On the other hand, works in which the chorus has a featured role give them incentive and spirit. Such an occasion was the Verdi Requiem of February 20, which was a Saturday-afternoon broadcast.

"Of course I would have liked more rehearsal, but we did sing it on tour last spring."

In the event, the chorus demonstrated its qualities of a unified yet distinct sound, attention to word and to meaning, and careful dynamics (indeed, the chorus paid more attention to dynamics than did the soloists). If the Requiem performance showed off the chorus as a whole, the *Oedipus Rex* performances showed off the male chorus (augmented by outsiders). Stivender has reason to be proud.

			F E B R U A R Y			
15	*16*	*17*	*18*	*19*	*20*	*20*
Il barbiere di Siviglia	**La Bohème**	**Così fan tutte**	**Il barbiere di Siviglia**	**La Bohème**	**Verdi Requiem**	**Così fan tutte**
Davis;	*Levine;*	*Levine;*	*Davis;*	*Tate;*	*Levine;*	*Levine;*
Horne,	*Zylis-Gara,*	*Te Kanawa,*	*Horne,*	*Zylis-Gara,*	*Price,*	*Lorengar,*
Blake,	*Migenes-*	*Battle,*	*Blake,*	*Migenes-*	*Quivar,*	*Battle,*
Elvira,	*Johnson,*	*Ewing,*	*Elvira,*	*Johnson,*	*Domingo,*	*Ewing,*
Dara,	*Domingo,*	*Rendall,*	*Dara,*	*Ciannella,*	*Cheek*	*Rendall,*
Berberian	*Ellis,*	*Morris,*	*Berberian*	*Ellis,*		*Carlson,*
	Monk,	*Gramm*		*Monk,*		*Gramm*
	Robbins			*Robbins*		

The Genteel Tradition

New productions define a Met season. In the absence of other factors—the appearances of star singers or conductors, unexpectedly spectacular debuts (such as Nilsson's in *Tristan*), or revivals of operas that, as performances, become almost as important as new productions (like this year's *Die Frau ohne Schatten* and *Tannhäuser*)—it is new productions that limn in the artistic profile of the company.

Virgil Thomson's dictum that whatever went on night after night at the Met, it was "not a part of New York's intellectual life" remains largely true, although Anthony Bliss argues that the attention given to out-of-the-way works such as *Parade*, the efforts of John Dexter, the designs of David Hockney, and even the added attractions of the spring and summer after the Met goes on tour (which in 1982 include the American Ballet Theatre, the Grand Kabuki of Japan, and the Royal Danish Ballet—all brought over under the Met's auspices, not by Lincoln Center) are a conscious effort to add a different element of excitement and make the Met "the talk of the town" apart from its standard core repertory. New music is only very infrequently performed at the Met, and though the current management has sought to put on the Met stage twentieth-century works such as *Mahagonny*, the *Parade* and Stravinsky triple bills, and *Lulu* (which should be in any respectable operatic repertory), it has also announced the indefinite postponement of *Moses und Aron*, which is a work built for the Met's spaces. It has done so, it says, because of the inordinate demands in rehearsal and staging that Schoenberg's opera requires; yet by that very token it is the Met, with its financial, artistic, and stage resources, that should confront these challenges as a matter of course, and not look to smaller-scale works because they are easier to perform, to sell, and to justify financially. Andrew Porter's contention about Bernd Alois Zimmermann's *Die Soldaten*—which in complexity makes *Moses und Aron* look like a kindergarten exercise—that "the Met or the City Opera should have undertaken [it] years ago, should have revived it regularly, and should have played it the length and breadth of the country" (*The New Yorker*, March 1, 1982) may be unrealistically idealistic, but it nonetheless contains more than a grain of truth.

"New opera" in the greater New York area was best represented in the fall of 1981 by Philip Glass's *Satyagraha*, performed at the Brooklyn Academy of Music. Whether that work is a legitimate contribution to opera or simply a transitory phenomenon, it represented something relatively new, something well set forward, and something, moreover, that appealed strongly to audiences. Although the Metropolitan Opera House was the site of Glass's earlier work (with Robert Wilson) *Einstein on the Beach*, it was not presented under Met auspices or as part of the season. Indeed, the Met has generally looked for audience appeal to older, more established operas, and was surprised when a venture such as 1981's *Parade* became a hit.

Similarly, the Met has not sought to provide an analogous contemporaneity through out-of-the-way stagings, except for the timid (by European standards) efforts of John Dexter. After the fiasco of the borrowed *Fliegende Holländer* production of 1979, the management has not sought to mount anything that might smack of outré adventurousness. The Met was known to be relieved when the labor difficulties canceled plans for a production of Tchaikovsky's *Pique Dame* to be directed by Rumania's Liviu Ciulei: there were rumors that his ideas about the opera were not those of the composer. A *Bohème* produced in an outsized production may not be quite what the composer had in mind, but it satisfies subscribers, attracts ticket buyers, and, though it causes a few grumbles, does not outrage. The extent of the Met's daring in staging is confined to such details as Colin Graham's decision, in *Così fan tutte*, to have the lovers pair off at final curtain fall as they did in the second act rather than go back to their first-act pairings. This last decision is not a small one in the context of the opera, as several critics noted, since the opera is all about a cynical wager that women can be persuaded by any man who comes along. Both women are—but are they? This ambiguity is "resolved" when the women are seen to stick to their new swains.

Still, it is a small enough point not to have been considered worthy of mention by the *Times*'s Donal Henahan in his review, and it is certainly one that passes unnoticed by the majority of the Met's audience. In the context of a largely traditional staging, these changes assume greater significance, but they are in no way comparable in effect to setting a Handel opera on Cape Canaveral or playing the final scene of *Aida* in a gas chamber.

And yet even the decision in favor of the traditional carries with it more than simply a flavor of stand-pat conservatism. Each opera exists on its own terms, within its own historical and performance confines, and each opera must be reinterpreted through the filter of today's, and not yesterday's, experience. To state that the Met, in 1981–82, gave new productions of one eighteenth-century opera, three nineteenth-century operas, and a group of twentieth-century works, each more or less "traditionally" performed, says little. The Met may not, in light of productions of opera elsewhere, be seen to have embraced a single style of production; and in contrast with the practices of theaters controlled by one dominant personality (e.g., Balanchine's New York City Ballet), the Met may indeed be accused of a heterogeneousness and an ad hoc approach. But to those who have observed the flux of productions over the last few years, there are threads that bind them together: threads that can be said to define many of the new productions seen in the house.

These threads go back to John Dexter. Dexter's productions of the nineteenth-century core repertory operas were generally considered his weakest, for various reasons; but constant in many of them was a streamlining, and constant in all of them was an attempt to present people rather than operatic types onstage. At least this was what Dexter said he wanted.

Paradoxically, however, what emerged from Dexter's various stagings—of the twentieth-century operas as well as the earlier works—has been not a greater involvement but a greater distancing. Dexter's stagings are defined by their almost total lack of human contact. They can be symbolized by his decision to play the final moments of *Rigoletto*—when the anguished jester is left alone onstage with the body of his beloved daughter, killed by another but in effect, as he realizes, killed by himself—as a light show of melodramatic flashes against the night sky, thus shifting the focus from Rigoletto to some sort of Grand Guignol macabre, devoid of personalized grief. "No tears!" Dexter once said to his cast.

Dexter's 1978 production of Donizetti's *Don Pasquale* is another example of this distancing. He transformed the tale of the older man (not a little overweight) who decides to take a wife into a comedy in the Oscar Wilde vein, moving up the time of the opera to conform to this viewpoint. In so doing, Dexter departed from the generalized Brechtian approach that he had introduced into other of his stagings and fell back on his native English tradition, which—up to John Osborne's *Look Back in Anger*—was solidly grounded in the middlebrow boulevard or drawing-room comedic writing, in exact tune with the sensibilities and tastes of a comfortable middle-class audience. Dexter substituted this British manner for Italian matter, and undercut what was central to that great comic opera. The result was pleasant—Don Pasquale became a handsome, debonair lepidopterist—and certainly avoided the broad comedy of earlier stagings; but it distorted Donizetti's opera. The plots fomented against this man by his nephew, his supposed wife, and his friend the doctor seemed capricious and cruel—he was just too nice; and besides, he was sophisticated enough to know what was going on. The original Pasquale is a figure out of commedia dell'arte: an oldster, not a little asinine and certainly pigheaded, who deserves his fate, but who, in that moment which gives the opera its stature beyond farce, suddenly becomes human and vulnerable, so that the audience swings into sympathy with his plight. Dexter's staging, however, left something out. It left out the heart.

This pervasive lack of human feeling was put into vivid relief by Gian Carlo Menotti's staging of Puccini's *Manon Lescaut* in 1980, for throughout that production Menotti made the audience believe in the immediacy of the love and loss of Manon and Des Grieux, so that Puccini's youthful score was reflected by the onstage passions of the characters.

This season, two productions—*Così* and *Il barbiere di Siviglia*—similarly sought to avoid the buffooneries sometimes associated with those operas. Again, the stated aim was to put real people rather than types onstage, and to watch them interact rather than overact. *Così* can more naturally accommodate itself to this environment, for its artifice and its equipoise between mask and face invite restraint. *Barbiere*, however, cannot.

Rossini's *Il barbiere di Siviglia* is one of the master buffo comedies in the repertory. It has withstood a century and a half of slapstick, coloratura excess, and egregious overacting, and it has always survived. It has survived because Rossini wrote for it some of the most ebullient and joyous music ever penned for opera.

For this production, director John Cox chose to take another view. "Who needs floppy hats, huge razors, mounds of shaving foam all over the stage?" he wrote in *Opera News* (March 13, 1982). "*The Barber* is a comedy of manners, all about elegant, civilized behavior. Its characters are comic, but the humor stems from their *reality*. I just hope that Maestro Davis will rein my cast in sufficiently to accommodate these purist ideas!"

And that is just what resulted: a reined-in, civilized, and elegant *Barber*, which was, to many, no *Barber* at all, but some London boulevard comedy set to Rossini's music.

All three of these directors—Dexter, Graham, and Cox—whatever their individual differences, are Englishmen working out of the background of the traditional English theater.

The impact of the English sensibility upon opera today has been too little written about. This is because it is far less immediately evident than the revolutionary changes of the French and German schools of opera directing. Yet in the United States, which has been far more tradition minded and conservative in its opera productions than has Europe, the impact of the English sensibility has been great.

This tradition stems from the small theater at Glyndebourne. There, founder John Christie, his original staff, and his successors imposed a kind of production concept—first on Mozart and then on the rest of the repertory—that emphasized a treatment of opera as a sung play, of people in real situations, and without the exaggerations of acting and vocal behavior that typified the then current and historic operatic style. It is no accident that John Cox was director of production at Glyndebourne for many years.

The "Glyndebourne style," however, was not confined to that theater, for the fame of that opera house led to its precepts spreading throughout the British Isles. The years since the Second World War and the first production of Britten's *Peter Grimes* (1945) have seen the dramatic rise of England as a home for opera, both for operas by native composers and for opera companies, and as a home for the training of opera singers and directors. Today, such different works as *Tristan und Isolde* and the *Ring* cycle are regularly performed, not only by the Royal Opera at Covent Garden (the international house), but by the English National Opera (in English) and the Welsh National Opera, to general critical acclaim. This rise in importance has been consciously abetted by the British press and by the strongly chauvinistic backing of the leading operatic critical review in the English-speaking world, the London-based *Opera* magazine under the editorship of Harold Rosenthal.

The fact that England has had, and continues to have, a tradition of spoken drama and opera in English has definitely influenced the production of its operas, for many of its top directors—Dexter, Jonathan Miller, Peter Hall—work in both mediums. Thus the aesthetics and practices of the theater are carried over into opera, and in this milieu, the antics of the parody-Italian tenor are looked on askance, if not laughed at as hopelessly outdated.

I remember speaking a few years ago to George Christie, the son of the founder of Glyndebourne and now himself in charge there, who was in New York on a visit. He was aghast at a Met performance of Donizetti's *L'elisir d'amore*. This production, it must be said, was some way from being new, but the original director, Nathaniel Merrill, had been on hand for its revival. Yet by Christie's Glyndebourne standards, that production was obvious, hammy, and overacted—precisely those qualities that Glyndebourne had sought to eliminate from its stagings. What in fact offended Christie most, I felt, was less these qualities than the production's essential and overweening vulgarity.

And this is the crux. The avoidance of any hint of the vulgar has indeed led to the avoidance of a lot of baggage usually associated with opera, particularly Italian opera; but it has also resulted in a kind of genteelism that, however well it works within the confines of Glyndebourne, becomes effete and pusillanimous on the stage of the Met. The gut exuberance that is integral to Rossini's *Barbiere* was gone, and through the pale sepia tones of Enzo Dara's Dr. Bartolo—nicely shaded, nicely calculated: nice—I heard the bass of Fernando Corena, who for many years owned the role at the Met (in the production of Cyril Ritchard, which banged the bass drum of buffoonery at sempre forte). Corena was a quintessential hambone buffo, and at times his performance chewed up everything in sight; but, by God, he was a presence, he could act, and he could sing. He wore his vulgarity with panache.

Insofar as any single production concept is seen at the Met, then, it is one derived from an English model. The Met perhaps cannot be called Covent Garden West, as Carol Fox's Lyric Opera of Chicago was called La Scala West; but the house employs a number of expatriate Englishmen and -women, including one assistant manager (Joan Ingpen) and one production advisor (John Dexter). This English influence has, in addition, resulted in one production detail that is, to some Americans, offensive. Elijah Moshinsky's production of Verdi's *Un ballo in maschera*—Moshinsky is English too, though born in Australia—updated the action to Boston on the eve of the American Revolution (he based the production on Dexter's ideas). Thus, the colonial governor, a loyalist, was the humane "good guy," and the reactionary villains(!), bent on assassination, were the fathers of the revolution (one of them was costumed as Sam Adams). This is not only a distortion of history, but a calumny.

What is more important, however, is that the Met, while consciously developing young American singers and conductors, is doing nothing about developing or presenting American stage directors. Since Nathaniel Merrill—hardly a major director—departed, no one has replaced him at the Met. More centrally, in the five seasons since 1978 (I include the 1982–83 season), the only "American" stage director employed for a new production was Gian Carlo Menotti, who, though an Italian citizen, can be considered at least quasi-American—and Menotti was brought in at a late date to substitute for an Englishman. Paradoxically, the Met's next American director, Frank Corsaro, who is scheduled to stage Handel's *Rinaldo* in the centennial season, comes to the Met in a production that is a gift from Canada!

Perhaps there are no American directors as qualified for the Met as Dexter, Ponnelle, Cox, Graham, Schenk, or Peter Hall; yet a house that is putting forward Malfitano, Battle, Rockwell Blake, or Lenus Carlson in major roles, and Thomas Fulton, Eugene Kohn, Lawrence Foster, and James Conlon as conductors, could extend its search to uncover one or two likely candidates.

The genteel tradition sits uneasily on the Met, despite certain successes. Insofar as it represents the artistic policy of the management, it serves to undercut that vitality and force that is endemic, for good or for ill, to opera.

			F E B R U A R Y			
22	23	24	25	26	27	27
La Bohème	**Così fan**	**Il barbiere**	**La Bohème**	**Il trovatore**	**Così fan**	**Il barbiere**
Levine;	**tutte**	**di Siviglia**	*Levine;*	*Conlon;*	**tutte**	**di Siviglia**
Zylis-Gara,	*Levine;*	*Davis;*	*Zylis-Gara,*	*Cruz-Romo,*	*Levine;*	*Davis;*
Migenes-	*Lorengar,*	*Horne,*	*Migenes-*	*Dunn,*	*Lorengar,*	*Horne,*
Johnson,	*Battle,*	*Blake,*	*Johnson,*	*Mauro,*	*Battle,*	*Blake,*
Domingo,	*Ewing,*	*Elvira,*	*Ciannella,*	*Quilico*	*Ewing,*	*Elvira,*
Ellis,	*Rendall,*	*Dara,*	*Ellis,*		*Rendall,*	*Dara,*
Sereni,	*Carlson,*	*Berberian*	*Sereni,*		*Carlson,*	*Berberian*
Robbins	*Gramm*		*Robbins*		*Gramm*	

They Also Serve Who Only Stand and Cheer

E very opera house of note is surrounded by a tribe of devotees of the cult. The vocal or opera buffs come in two kinds: those who prefer to live on recorded memories and those who live through live performances. The Met has its share of both kinds. The second kind, of course, is the kind most in evidence at performances, and can be typified by Lois Kirschenbaum ("Miss Cherry Tree, as Jon Vickers calls me"), the queen of the Met regulars.

Kirschenbaum, a thin, intense woman who wears heavy eyeglasses because of poor sight and on opera nights carries a big pair of binoculars, is indeed a regular. She grew up in Brooklyn, where (naturally) she was a devoted Dodgers fan; but a few years before the Bums decamped for greener, if hardly less smog-filled, pastures—perhaps Kirschenbaum subliminally sensed the future— she happened to hear a recording of *La Bohème* with Renata Tebaldi. "I never imagined such sounds could come from the human throat." By the time the Dodgers left town, Kirschenbaum had become an opera fanatic, and she has enlarged on her passion ever since.

"One day I was playing a record and my father came in and said, 'That's Caruso—I heard him, you know.' He had heard Caruso and Gigli and Chaliapin, but he had never told me—my mother never liked opera. Today he's eighty-four, and doesn't go to the Met, but now and then he sees it on television. Can you imagine—he heard Caruso live!"

By day Kirschenbaum is a telephone receptionist, and as such she acts in two capacities: that of her business and that of coordinator of the network of opera buffs of her acquaintance. After five, however, she heads for music. Almost every night, and twice on Saturdays and Sundays, Kirschenbaum is at a musical event. She is at the Met, during its season, three or four times a week ("depending on the schedule—sometimes it's less"); if not there, at the New York City Opera, at the ballet, or at concerts and recitals. "Sometimes I even get to the theater or the movies."

Since she has a limited amount of money, she often obtains free tickets or discount tickets, in ways known to all music lovers but which she is reluctant to discuss. For the Met, however, since she has little time to wait for standing room (sold at ten on the morning of the performance*), Kirschenbaum arranges her season before the house opens and purchases score desk seats (the cheapest in the house) for all the performances she knows she wants.

"It's a lot of money for me to lay out, but then I don't have to worry about getting in."

Once inside the Met, she can usually find an empty seat somewhere with a view of the stage, and sometimes a critic with an extra seat will let her have it. "The ushers are very nice, but recently they've been cracking down, because some people—I don't know who they are—have been taking subscribers' seats and refusing to move out when the ticket holders come."

Kirschenbaum's evening does not end with the final curtain fall.

---

*This policy was changed in 1982–83.

She always goes backstage ("except if I can get a ride home and they won't wait") to congratulate the artists and get them to sign her program or photographs.

"Sometimes I don't get on the subway until almost one o'clock in the morning, if it's a Wagner opera. I'm so glad Jimmy moved the *Tannhäuser* curtain to seven-thirty next year! A few nights ago I was so tired I could hardly stay awake for the last act—you don't know how wearing it is, if you have to get up every day to go to a job!"

Kirschenbaum goes to the opera primarily for the voices. Her special interest lies in following young American artists in their rising careers, often from City Opera to the Met. "I saw Judith Raskin go up the ladder, and now I'm seeing Kathleen Battle. I grow up with them."

Although she likes to see different artists in different roles, she is in favor of the current management's policy of broadening the operatic repertory. "When I first heard *Mahagonny*, on the radio, I didn't like it. When I saw it in the opera house, I liked Stratas and some of the music. But it grew on me, and I can understand why they did it. It will never be my favorite opera—and *Lulu* won't be, either—but you have to give these things a chance, if they're done as well as they do them at the Met."

Her favorite opera is *Die Frau ohne Schatten*—if it is well cast— and her second favorite is Boito's *Mefistofele*, a staple at the City Opera but unheard since the 1920s at the Met. "After that first *Frau* I was walking on air! I never imagined opera could be like this!"

But, night after night, her favorites remain the Italian operas— Verdi, Bellini, Puccini—and she remains cool to Wagner, in part because of the lack of Wagnerian singers.

Kirschenbaum is firmly committed to the policies of the current management and is a strong supporter of the music director. "It's much more relaxed at the Met than in the Bing days. Can you imagine Bing speaking to me? But I can talk to Jimmy about anything, when I see him after the opera, and he always gives me direct answers. There are no airs with him. The prima donna era of opera is fading: everyone is more relaxed, and there is an ensemble spirit that wasn't there before."

She is enthusiastic about Levine's conducting. "He's learning all the time, and he gets better and better. His Verdi is tops. I know he gets some bad press, and they say he conducts too much, but one thing: Jimmy will never put you to sleep with his conducting. He's a brilliant conductor, and an unassuming pal."

Levine also gives her a ticket now and then to performances, such as the Domingo/Troyanos concert that was planned after the season began.

Kirschenbaum prefers to sit upstairs if she has the choice. "You can't imagine the difference in sound. The worst seats are under the overhang in the orchestra—I'll never sit there."

Kirschenbaum is part of a large group of opera devotees, all of whom dote on the ins and outs of performances at the Met. She knows the casts of operas for years ahead—up to the 1985–86 season—and sometimes she knows of cast changes even before the management. (Indeed, her fund of information, and at times misinformation, is the source of some annoyance to those backstage.)

Kirschenbaum maintains that though some singers have fan clubs who appear in order to cheer, the paid claque, once endemic to an opera house, is a thing of the past.

"One of my dislikes is people who can't contain themselves, and who applaud during the high note, or before the music ends. I loved it when the audience shushed the people before the curtain in *Bohème*, so that you could hear the last notes."

Kirschenbaum hasn't much to say about the ticket scalpers who are present at star evenings, since she disdains those who make money off the Met but never go inside to see the opera.

One recognizable figure who does go inside, but is more often seen outside—beside the right-hand entrance to the opera house—is the ubiquitous Monte, in his variety of fedoras and, for big evenings, his buttonhole flower.

Monte is used by subscribers and others who do not want to turn in their extra tickets for resale at the box office (no refund is ever given; the money goes to the Pension Fund); he will undertake to flack tickets for those who are not expert in the art. For this valuable service, he receives whatever tip the person cares to give him.

Monte is a Met legend, and his outdoor patter before a performance is an integral part of the Met experience. One Saturday afternoon, he was expatiating:

"I have two excellent center-orchestra seats—thirty dollars each, only as a pair, don't ask me for one—for *Vespro siciliano*. Come on: it's a great show! Who wants them? Two tickets! Don't ask me for tonight—THERE ARE NO TICKETS FOR TONIGHT! The house is completely sold out—no tickets anywhere, not even standing room! Come on, two orchestra for this afternoon—you can't go wrong."

Monte accepts tickets to resell for future performances, and apparently his honor system works. "I have no telephone," he told one prospective buyer, "but I'm usually here before a performance."

He usually is, too, though on big nights at Carnegie Hall or the City Opera or the Philharmonic he is there, and I once saw him directing traffic for the nonexistent traffic cop at the busy intersection of Fifty-seventh Street and Madison Avenue.

One opera devotee, who gets to New York on business at irregular intervals, almost never buys tickets through mail order or at the box office. "I get a better selection outside. If I know I'll be free that evening, I'll go over to the Met and can almost always get in—extra singles are pretty easy to get. Except on the biggest nights, the idea that you can't get into the Met is a myth."

Kirschenbaum tends to blame the vicissitudes of casting on Joan Ingpen; she doesn't consider that Bliss has any role except on the financial side. When she has a few spare moments, she listens to records of old singers at home: "my darling Supervia, or Boninsegna, or Ponselle." But she rarely sees retired singers (unlike some cultists); she prefers to patronize the up-and-coming ones. "One night I had to chase Kathleen Battle for a whole block to get her autograph."

As can be imagined, Kirschenbaum's apartment in lower Manhattan is jammed with memorabilia: programs, newspaper and magazine cuttings, photographs ("They even borrowed some from me for the book on Tebaldi"), and lapel buttons sporting photos of opera stars. "I'm a saver—it's a sickness almost, but I can't throw anything away.

"New York is a mecca—there's everything for everybody. I can't imagine living anywhere else. At odd times I try to fit in some theater, but the Met is my first home. It should be—I'm home a lot less than I'm at the Met!

"We're all of us at the Met because we love opera. The human voice is the greatest instrument, and I'm happy when I see a singer become famous at the Met. In the centennial year there will be the debuts of Jessye Norman, Samuel Ramey, and Carol Vaness—all Americans. I can't wait!"

Kirschenbaum is not a single-minded fan of one singer to the exclusion of others; but neither is she entirely undiscriminating. About one Met cast she said, "I don't think I'll go to hear *them*," yet it was said not angrily, but with a certain resignation. She realizes that in a repertory season, there will inevitably be nights when the amount charged for the ticket is not commensurate with the artistic value received. On those nights, she will be elsewhere.

If Kirschenbaum is a groupie, then she is a groupie for opera, and as such she and her loyal cohorts are an indispensable adjunct to the ongoing vitality of a night in the opera house. And if you want to know the latest gossip (true or false), just call her up.

M   A   R   C   H

1	2	3	4	5	6	6
Così fan tutte	**Il trovatore**	**La traviata**	**Così fan tutte**	**Il trovatore**	**La traviata**	**Il barbiere di Siviglia**
Levine;	_Conlon;_	_Rescigno;_	_Tate;_	_Conlon;_	_Rescigno;_	_Davis;_
Lorengar,	_Cruz-Romo,_	_Malfitano,_	_Lorengar,_	_Cruz-Romo,_	_Malfitano,_	_Horne,_
Battle,	_Dunn,_	_M. Cortez,_	_Battle,_	_Dunn,_	_Rendall,_	_Blake,_
Ewing,	_Mauro,_	_MacNeil_	_Ewing,_	_Bini,_	_MacNeil_	_Elvira,_
Rendall,	_Quilico_		_Rendall,_	_Quilico_		_Dara,_
Carlson,			_Carlson,_			_Berberian_
Gramm			_Gramm_			

Second Performances

I t was said best by Leighton Kerner: "It's a plain matter of common sense to go back to a performance, rehear a new score, walk once more through an art exhibition, and otherwise reassess. . . . New productions in an opera house the size of the Met almost invariably deserve rehearing and re-viewing, particularly from different vantage points. The upstairs and downstairs audiences sometimes hear a different performance because orchestral sound gets louder in relation to voices when heard from on high. Visual differences can be more marked, depending on how the director and designer treat stage depth, blocking and sightlines. Also, performances tend to improve with time, all other factors being equal, and when factors such as singers or conductor change it can be a whole new ballgame."*

---

*Kerner's words appear in the January 19, 1982, _Village Voice_. The entire review, which details various performances of the Stravinsky triple bill, is well worth reading.

Opera, no less than any performance art, varies with each performance, and those variations may cardinally affect the result. If the Met management's most reiterated complaint is that no one says that, night after night, the Met performs on a higher level than any other comparable repertory house in the world, its second complaint is that it is being judged on the basis of one performance out of many of a given opera and cast. This complaint carries with it an element of truth. New productions especially are best seen and heard at second or third performances, but those are not the ones most journalistic critics attend. All too often, front-line critics, because of the number of other performances of music in New York requiring reviews, do not see a representative cross-section of performances at the Met, and thus they base their summational Sunday pieces on "the Met season" on only a partial acquaintance with the product, as seen exclusively from seats in the orchestra.

The amount of variation from performance to performance is today perhaps smaller than in times past, because of the fewer changes in cast, fewer one-night stands by singers, and a greater effort by the management to arrive at a singleness of ensemble. Yet even small variations can shift and color a performance to influence the final estimate and the final enjoyment. Each performance—each of the two hundred and ten in the 1981–82 season—thus stands on its own, as any regular operagoer can attest. It is an understood, and common, disclaimer about the relativity of performances that to say "But you must have heard it on another night" is an acceptable excuse. (At times, however, the "other" performance happens to be the same one, leading to the time-honored line about music criticism: "We were both in the same house, but we heard different performances.")

The *Traviata* I heard on March 12 was an excellent example. I had, as may be remembered, heard the opera at the beginning of the season, at which time it was reviewed in the press. It went out of the repertory on November 2 and returned on March 3. This practice used to be quite usual, depending upon the availability of singers. An opera might be done once or twice, then not for two weeks or more. But today, in its semi-stagione format, the Met

tries not to do this. But the exigencies of the broadcast season
demand twenty operas in twenty broadcasts; and since the season
is over two months old when the broadcasts begin, one or more
operas may have to be "brought back," either for a broadcast or
for reacquaintance by the cast if an opera is to be taken on tour.
(*Norma* was brought back for two performances in one week, one
a broadcast.) Three operas presented in September and October—*Die Frau ohne Schatten, Das Rheingold,* and *Siegfried*—finished
their runs before the broadcast season began.

In the March 12 performance, the Alfredo and the Germont
were not the singers I had heard in the fall, but the Violetta was
still Catherine Malfitano. Malfitano's Violetta has divided opinion
to a greater extent than usual. Some consider her a fine, almost a
great Violetta; others feel that she is provincial in enunciation and
stage deportment and lacking in voice for that role, and that she
should not be a first-cast Met Violetta. It is true that Malfitano
lacks that prima donna sureness and vocal amplitude that define
major singing in a major opera house: she is neither a Callas nor
a Sutherland. Yet she possesses very real fragility of demeanor, a
feeling for the character, and a voice that, while never a dominating force, can nonetheless encompass the demands of the role,
and can suggest its pathos in a way that Sutherland, for instance,
never could.

I tried to fit her March performance into my memory of her
earlier one. The later one seemed even more assured in its specifics, although she kept to the same general blocking; and in the last
act she somewhat toned down her movements. The final scene of
Traviata is a test for any actress: Violetta dying of consumption in
despair, the arrival of her lover, Alfredo, and her consequent fe-
verish excitement of joy and hope, followed by relapse, a momen-
tary "cure"—and death. Malfitano obviously had thought the se-
quence through, and where in the first performance she had
emphasized the nervous mania of the character, by the reprise she
had coordinated that febrility into an overall and coherent progress.
Yet what was notable about both performances was the naturalness
of her responses. Although Malfitano was essentially doing the

same things onstage as when I saw her before, she gave the impression of creating Violetta anew for that night. There was never a sense of rote or of routine. The tendency of the management to cast for type worked here to advantage.

But the cardinal difference between that evening and the earlier one lay in the conducting of Nicola Rescigno. Here the value of the "second performance" proved itself. Had I been blindfolded, or not read his name in the program, I would have insisted there was another conductor in the pit.

Rescigno is known as a singers' conductor—he was a favorite of Callas's—but the performances I have heard from him at the Met have been anything but the work of such a type. They have been stiff, obdurate, working against rather than with the singers, rarely bringing out the flow of the music, and often—anathema for a singers' conductor—out of synchronization with those onstage. In September, he and Malfitano seemed on differing wavelengths, and time and again he inhibited her performance by not enhancing her phrasing and her subtle tempo variations with his orchestral accompaniment. My companion left in the first intermission.

That performance was on the third night of the season, and the orchestra had spent its time rehearsing other music (*Norma, Rheingold,* and *Siegfried*). *Traviata* had been performed at the end of the last season and on tour, but not with Rescigno. Doubtless Rescigno's allotted rehearsal time had been insufficient for his needs: I assume he is the type of conductor who must have time to feel his way into a score, even a score he knows well, and cannot, like some disciplinarians, arrive and will a performance from his players. By March 12 he had an autumn run of *Traviata*s behind him, and three more of the spring run. He knew the production and its demands. His music making was now at one with his singers, and he shaped the performance far better. He now matched the natural flow that Malfitano provided. (This experience calls into question the idea that just because an opera has been done in the spring or on tour, it needs less rehearsal when it is brought back in the autumn.)

The fascination of opera in performance is encapsulated in this experience. Unlike movies and records, each performance can be varied, and a single performance can even vary from act to act. This kind of variation—or the expectation of variation—is what brings people to the opera house again and again, for operas that have been heard many times. One night Placido Domingo sang Alvaro in *La forza del destino* as well as I have heard the role sung, yet another performance later in the run was much less accomplished. On another night, Linda Zoghby debuted by stepping into the role of Mimi in *La Bohème* on short notice and sang it well enough to earn a standing ovation. It is an integral part of the magic of repertory opera.

			MARCH			
8	9	10	11	12	13	13
Les Contes d'Hoffmann	**La traviata**	**Il barbiere di Siviglia**	**Les Contes d'Hoffmann**	**La traviata**	**Il barbiere di Siviglia**	**Il trovatore**
Chailly;	Rescigno;	Davis;	Chailly;	Rescigno;	Davis;	Conlon;
Welting,	Malfitano,	Battle,	Welting,	Malfitano,	Battle,	Amara,
Eda-Pierre,	M. Cortez,	Blake,	Eda-Pierre,	M. Cortez,	Blake,	V. Cortez,
Troyanos,	Ellis	Elvira,	Troyanos,	Ellis	Workman,	Bini,
Howells,		Capecchi,	Howells,		Capecchi,	Clark
Domingo,		Montarsolo	Domingo,		Montarsolo	
Devlin			Devlin			

French Opera and Opera Editions

Monday, March 8 saw the premiere, in a second Guild benefit, of the season's final new production, Offenbach's *Les Contes d'Hoffmann*. Every subsequent performance was sold out, with lines waiting for return tickets and would-be buyers imploring tickets from Met-goers a block away from the opera house.

The Met's grand staircase (a gift in memory of Robert Walton Goelet) was dolled up in blue-and-white striped awnings for a "Venetian Festival" dinner—one act of the opera is set in that city—inappropriately devoted to roast beef. Sprays of forsythia celebrated the long-awaited arrival of spring (somewhat prematurely: a month later I went to a meeting at the Met through a blizzard). Television cameras were also in the foyer, because the evening's star singer, Placido Domingo, had the week before graced the cover of *Newsweek* in an article entitled "King of the Opera." (King of the Opera last year was Luciano Pavarotti. And I remember a matinee *Otello* with Mario del Monaco in the old house, at a time when the Met still permitted draping of banners in the auditorium, much as is done at sporting events; that day, one such banner read "Il re dei tenori.")

Offenbach's posthumous work—his only "opera," as opposed to the many operettas he wrote—was also the only French opera of the repertory season.

French opera, in almost all opera houses, is a neglected area of the repertory. One reason is the lack of top-rate French operatic composers who wrote a body of work, as Verdi, Wagner, Mozart, and Puccini did. Although it seems that every French composer felt compelled to write an opera at some point in his career, extremely few of the resultant works have held the stage. The major French operatic composers have been very few: Rameau, Berlioz, Bizet. But Rameau is difficult to produce, Berlioz's stagecraft was never his strong suit, and *Carmen* is the only really finished product of Bizet's abbreviated career—and that opera is fraught with problems. Debussy's *Pelléas et Mélisande* is esteemed by the elite and ignored by the public, though Levine keeps it on the fringes of the repertory. And much of the rest of the short list of popular French operas, such as *Faust* and *Manon,* are dismissed with the epithet "good of their kind." Sir Thomas Beecham's remark that he would trade in the Brandenburg concertos for *Manon* and feel he had got much the best of the bargain has always been considered an amusing eccentricity of a playful mind.

Another reason for the neglect of French opera is the lack of French singers. It is very dangerous to try to define a national singing style, for all great singers will transcend the limits of the style. But it can be said that what is peculiar to French opera in general is an attention to the enunciation of the text, for language and word are considered more important in France than in Italy and Germany. This is because of the strong French tradition of spoken drama, which from the first carried over into opera and which over the centuries has retained its force.

Though numerous French operas have been composed in what could be termed an international style, dependent upon voice over enunciation (*Faust, Samson et Dalila,* the warhorses of Meyerbeer), there is a genre of French operas that gain immeasurably from being understood (Charpentier's *Louise* and, an extreme example, Satie's *Socrate*). Massenet's operas can be performed in the international style, but in his writing the words have colored the music written for them, which then highlights the words. To look at Massenet's scores (and those of predecessors such as Ambroise Thomas) is to see a forest of hairpin dynamics and sudden shifts from soft to loud singing, which always enhance the text and bring it alive musically. Ideally, the singer should phrase these indicia in a natural, and never mannered, way: by so doing he or she brings out the meaning of the text expressively. But it is always easier to ignore the indications and to give a generalized reading.

Thirdly, it is an indisputable fact that, though Paris in the eighteenth and nineteenth centuries was an operatic center, and even at times a center of music in general, the French have never really embraced music as they have theater, spectacle, and intrigue. It is indicative that two of France's most characteristic composers, Berlioz and the transplanted German Offenbach, are having their complete works published by firms outside France,* while her most famous opera, *Carmen,* is best known to the learned fraternity in the highly controversial and massive edition of Fritz Oeser, published in Germany by the same firm, Bärenreiter, that also published *Margarethe* (the German title for *Faust*) and *Les Contes d'Hoffmann.*

The disappearance from the repertory of most French operas of the nineteenth and early twentieth centuries, except for fitful attempts at revival, has confirmed the secondary status of the genre; so has the lack of contemporary French operas of note, in direct contradistinction to the outpouring of new operas in England. This situation has probably led to the diminution of the number of French singers and the internationalization of its remaining repertory. In the 1920s and 1930s such singers as

---

*The New Berlioz Edition, like the old one, is being published in Germany, with an editorial board made up largely of English and American musicologists; the Offenbach edition is being published in the United States.

Germaine Lubin, Ninon Vallin, and Georges Thill enlivened the French repertory with their artistry: today, the most notable Carmens, Manons, Fausts, Josés, Samsons, Didos, and Enées are, with the single exception of Régine Crespin, of non-French origin. In the current *Les Contes d'Hoffmann* the only native French voice in the cast was that of Michel Sénéchal in the four comic roles; and although the Antonia, Christiane Eda-Pierre, came from the French island of Martinique, it was left to Sénéchal to define the special qualities of elegance and diction that have typified the form.

Les Contes d'Hoffmann raises the question of the performing edition. This question was once considered unimportant. In an age that wanted to hear the works and the singers (not necessarily in that order), fidelity to the text as the composer envisioned it was not addressed. Arias and ensembles were repeated if applause warranted, singers "broke character" to advance to stage front and bow after a big aria (a practice that still takes place at the Vienna Staatsoper, except on festival nights), and all sorts of interpolations were permitted—of extra arias, arias written for a particular production, even arias written by other composers (the lesson scene in *Il barbiere di Siviglia* became a parade ground of the soprano's most effective hits—Beverly Sills, in the 1976 New York City Opera revival, incorporated Adolphe Adam's variations on the tune we know as "Twinkle, twinkle, little star"). For many generations, the last scene of Bellini's *I Capuleti e i Montecchi* was not Bellini's but Zaccai's, which was thought to be better music.

With the greater attention now being paid to what the composer wrote, however, many of these almost automatic retouchings were called into question and discarded. Moreover, as the repertory concentrated ever more heavily on works of the past, there came hand in hand a desire to do right by the work and a desire to hear something new with the old: and not a spurious addition, but, if possible, one at least partly justified by history—a section cut during rehearsal, or an alternate version of an aria. An opera like Verdi's *Don Carlos,* which exists in several editions, can be performed in a half-dozen ways, all with some claim to authenticity. Thus the static repertory became enlarged.

It is very easy to decide to perform an opera as the composer wrote it, but it is sometimes inordinately difficult to arrive at just what that was. Opera by its very nature has always been a compromise art, with composers at the mercy of managements, singers, and deadlines, all of which affected the operatic result. Even after the premiere there were changes, to suit the tastes of another city or because the composer had other thoughts. Thus the printed score is not necessarily the final repository of authenticity.

These problems are of minimal interest to the average operagoer (and in general to the opera buff), but they are nonetheless vital to the artistic health of a repertory company, for they accurately reflect the measure of seriousness with which the company addresses its task of being a museum of the great and not-so-great works of the past rather than simply a singer's house or a circus. Virgil Thomson's quote about the Met not being part of New York's intellectual life, then, must to an extent be modified, for under music director James Levine the company has consciously tried to present productions that are musically and musicologically faithful. (Not all critics, however, feel that this should be so. One of them, defending cuts—even in the *Ring*—and other time-honored streamlining practices, said, "The Met is not a home of scholarly effort," implying that the show, and not the intent, is the thing.)

This is not an easy task, for it involves a host of details that earlier managements ignored. As in the area of translation, singers—particularly Met-caliber singers—are loath to learn a part anew. (At least two major bassos refuse to perform Mussorgsky's *Boris Godunov* in anything but the now scorned Rimsky-Korsakov edition.) The opening of cuts in a score is resisted, sometimes because a singer does not want to learn the additional music, sometimes because that music is difficult to sing. The easier (and less expensive) course is to give the opera in its standard form, particularly when more than one cast is involved.

In some cases there exists more than one "correct" version of an opera. Gluck's *Orfeo ed Euridice,* for instance, exists in two distinct versions written for different cities, both supervised by the composer, as well as in later versions by other hands. *Tannhäuser* exists in the original Dresden version and the later Paris one, expanded and to an extent altered by Wagner for the disastrous Paris premiere. Things become much more complicated with *Boris Godunov* and achieve dizzying complexity with *Carmen*. Bizet died shortly after the opera's premiere; and his final thoughts, whatever they were, are evidenced only in a few final letters and in the music he wrote, some of which was cut in rehearsal—but did he approve of these cuts, or simply acquiesce? For the subsequent Vienna premiere, Bizet was preparing to write recitatives in place of the spoken dialogue—would he have incorporated them into the opera permanently, or kept it as it was? Because of *Carmen's* stature, the tempests in this particular teapot achieve hurricane proportions, and any decision as to version must take into account these and many other considerations, some not musicological. (For example: if the company decides on spoken dialogue, can the singers perform it well enough to justify the choice? Might it not be preferable to perform the opera in the standard version, with the Ernest Guiraud recitatives, which most singers know and which they may be able to put across with greater impact?)

Les Contes d'Hoffmann carries this a step further, for Offenbach died before the opera was finished. Thus, the sketches for what he wanted were put into the hands of others, notably Guiraud, who arrived at a version premiered in Paris. Later, others added more Offenbach music—notably, Dapertutto's diamond aria in the Venice act, which has since become such a hit that only with force can it be prized from its setting.

Offenbach's methods of working, moreover, were those of a composer involved in profit-making theater. Like Broadway musical composers, he cut and changed right up to the premiere and even after opening night, rethinking the operetta constantly with a view to performance success as well as artistic necessity. All this was denied him in the case of *Hoffmann*.

Les Contes d'Hoffmann exists in the traditional score, published by the French firm Choudens; in the score by Fritz Oeser, published by Bärenreiter in Germany—more a musicological compilation than a performing score; and in various performing editions, notably those of Offenbach scholar Antonio de Almeida, of Richard Bonynge, and of James Levine and Jean-Pierre Ponnelle.

Levine did not conduct the opera at the Met (he currently conducts it in Salzburg), and even though he is music director, he was unable to impose any caveats on the production. Thus, his only instruction to the team of Günther Schneider-Siemssen (sets), Otto Schenk (direction), and Riccardo Chailly (conductor) was to put the opera on in such a way that if Levine decided to conduct it in future years, he could perform it in another version if he chose. (This is not an idle request. In the current production of *Fidelio* the set change between the dungeon scene and the final scene is complicated enough so that either there must be an intermission—counterindicated at this dramatic point—or the time-honored but non-Beethovenian interpolation of the third *Leonore* overture must be played.) Schenk decided to perform *Les Contes d'Hoffmann* in the standard Choudens version.

Although that decision hardly represented the kind of artistic fidelity the company has insisted upon in operas conducted by Levine, its justification lay in the fact that the edition was familiar, that it did not place an undue burden on the tenor, Placido Domingo (who had just sung the role in that edition at Covent Garden), and that the score itself is hardly of the stature of a *Carmen*.

Yet this last should not be used as an excuse for taking the easier path. If an opera is good enough to be performed at the Met, it should be treated with the same respect accorded *Meistersinger*. The Choudens edition may seriously misrepresent what Offenbach wrote: it is an adaptation, contains music Offenbach never intended to be in the score (the diamond aria) and music he never wrote (the so-called septet in the Venice act). Domingo, moreover, unlike most tenors, is flexible and a demon for work—among singers he is the counterpart of Levine, a perpetual motion machine. He might have welcomed the chance to perform yet another version of a role that is and has been one of his finest.

I could not help thinking, however, as I watched the marvelously crafted antics of the Olympia act, in the splendidly detailed inventor's workshop devised by that stage magician Schneider-Siemssen, that *Les Contes d'Hoffmann* was being performed because it is a rattling good theater piece loaded with tunes, and that the furthest thing from anyone's mind was having to worry about editions, inclusions, and deletions, or whether the Venice act comes second or third. And the audiences, packing the opera house to the walls, obviously agreed.

M   A   R   C   H

15	16	17	18	19	20	20
Les Contes d'Hoffmann	**Il barbiere di Siviglia**	**I vespri siciliani**	**La traviata**	**Il barbiere di Siviglia**	**I vespri siciliani**	**Les Contes d'Hoffmann**
Chailly;	*Davis;*	*Levine;*	*Rescigno;*	*Davis;*	*Levine;*	*Chailly;*
Bradley,	*Battle,*	*Scotto,*	*Malfitano,*	*Battle,*	*Scotto,*	*Welting,*
Malfitano,	*Gonzalez,*	*Ochman,*	*M. Cortez,*	*Gonzalez,*	*Ochman,*	*Eda-Pierre,*
Troyanos,	*Workman,*	*Elvira,*	*Ellis*	*Workman,*	*Elvira,*	*Troyanos,*
Howells,	*Capecchi,*	*Raimondi*		*Capecchi,*	*Raimondi*	*Howells,*
Domingo,	*Montarsolo*			*Montarsolo*		*Domingo,*
Devlin						*Devlin*

The Orchestra

On March 17, Verdi's little-performed opera *I vespri siciliani* entered the repertory. It had not been performed for some years; and even though it was a revival and not a new production, Levine and his chorus director, David Stivender, had set aside extra rehearsal time to prepare the work. *Vespri* is a "grand opera" involving top-notch singing and much choral work; its difficulties are significant, and are compounded by the fact that the work is, despite its apologists, not one of Verdi's strongest. John Dexter's production, moreover, was out of the ordinary in that the sets of Josef Svoboda consisted of staircases lit by white raking light; thus the cast had to become accustomed to working on unfamiliar terrain.

Since *Vespri* is a "grand opera," it requires more of the orchestra than do most nineteenth-century repertory operas.

An opera orchestra is an anomalous animal, for it is both necessary and secondary. It is necessary to give the singers support and to flesh out the music the composer wrote; it is secondary—unless the horn player fluffs—because the focus is onstage and not in the pit. Wagner brought the opera orchestra out of the dark ages, or so some historians say, but in fact composers long previous to the Magician had written demanding music for opera orchestra: Mozart and Beethoven, for two.

The growth of the opera orchestra has already been detailed to some extent in an earlier chapter. Today the orchestra is an integral part of the artistic makeup of any major opera house. With the appointment of a music director at the Met, the company orchestra began an upward journey which continues every season.

The Met's history began with its orchestra relegated to a minor position vis-à-vis the singers, although the Met boasted some fine conductors in its early years. The appearance of Mahler and Toscanini may have improved matters, as did the appearance of a number of exiled major conductors during the years of the Second World War and thereafter. Yet what is more accurate is that for many years between the wars the Met was the province of a few trained opera conductors (e.g., Artur Bodanzky, Tullio Serafin, and Ettore Panizza) who defined the type of ensemble repertory conducting Erich Leinsdorf spoke of earlier. Later on, Fausto Cleva carried on in that spirit, as did, more sporadically, Leinsdorf himself; but it is generally true that lacking that kind of ongoing Kapellmeister tradition, and only occasionally playing under top-flight maestros, the Met in the later Bing years floundered.

There is no doubt that the appointment of a music director who has taken over a great share of the repertory has had a significant impact on the orchestra. Here (as with John Dexter and his production work) one must separate two facets of the endeavor: Levine's conducting as heard in the opera house and his talents as an orchestra builder and enlivening presence. And whatever one may feel about James Levine's work in the pit, he has transformed those who must play seven times a week for thirty weeks.

Orchestra players may come to the profession because of a love for music or a love for playing their instruments; but the drudgery of playing over a span of weeks and years—and, in the case of an opera orchestra player, playing largely the same repertory—takes its inevitable toll. Routine sets in, the notes become rote, and the attitude is to get out of the opera house as soon as possible. (I remember, in times past, seeing an orchestra player lean over and kiss the final page of *Götterdämmerung*.)

Yet performing opera, rather than symphonic music, has its rewards. An opera orchestra, since it has to accompany singers and is subject to the many vicissitudes of stage performance, must possess a greater degree of flexibility and alertness than a symphony orchestra. To that extent, then, each performance of *La traviata* is created anew in a way that each performance of Beethoven's Fifth Symphony may not be. To an opera orchestra player this flexibility becomes second nature, and this kind of playing can invest the performance with spontaneity. The great symphony orchestras are all vulnerable to the charge that, good as they are in whatever qualities particular to them, at the highest level their expertise can become machinelike, with the technique exhibited for its own sake rather than at the service of the music. I do not think that can ever be said of any opera orchestra in the world, La Scala and Vienna included.

Any orchestra—opera, symphonic, or chamber—breaks down into players performing for their checks, players performing for the love of music, and players performing because they respond to the resident conductor. Each of the great conductors had in his orchestra a group of players dedicated to his way of making music (Toscanini surely, but even such other taskmasters as Szell and Reiner), and that dedication made itself felt to others in the orchestra—even to those who hated the maestro but, by God, would show him by playing their best.

Michael Ouzounian, the principal viola of the Met orchestra, is a Levine loyalist. He came to the Met in 1972 before he had finished his schooling, choosing the Met over an offer by the Pittsburgh Symphony because he loved opera. Many—but not all—opera orchestra members choose opera because of an affinity for the form; and though Ouzounian says that he could easily adapt to a symphonic milieu, he currently finds greater challenge and reward in playing for opera. Shortly after he arrived, Levine was made music director, and this event has kept Ouzounian at the Met.

"I don't think I could have survived more than four years in the orchestra as it was when I arrived," he said. "Everyone played for themselves, and there wasn't that collective pride that I find indispensable for my work."

Ouzounian is totally convinced of the greatness of the music director, and admires his methods of rehearsal. "Levine is never negative, and he often lets pass mistakes that someone else may stop and correct, simply because he knows the player is aware of them. Some conductors like to instill a negative competitiveness in an orchestra in order to get results, but I find that if this is done I tend to get negative myself, and downgrade the playing of others instead of trying to build up an ensemble sense."

Ouzounian greatly enjoys playing opera. "I think it's a more creative possibility than symphonic playing. At first, you see that the notes are easy and the patterns often monotonous, but you soon get over these value judgments. Their ease means that you can explore the expressive possibilities further."

Ouzounian feels that the orchestra he is a part of is improving year by year, not as much because there is a music director in the house as because there is this particular music director. "And this change has been done without many changes in the orchestra, at least in the string section. I find that the players are listening to each other more, and there is an ensemble sensitivity there wasn't before."

Even allowing for Ouzounian's bias, the marked improvement of the Met orchestra is evident, certainly on the nights that Levine conducts. Specifics can be indicated. Orchestral balance is better, so that the brass does not dominate, and string attacks and chordings are more precise. (The chordings in this year's *Parsifal* were exquisitely rendered: the thirds and the fifths shimmering in the sound, distinct yet integrated.) The orchestra sounds like a many-voiced whole, with woodwind phrases not played note by note but phrased from beginning to end, emerging from the orchestral context and being subsumed into it. Since each principal orchestral player has an individual sound, the danger of opposing timbres is always present. For instance, principal cellist Jascha Silberstein tends toward very romantic playing of his instrument (Robert Lawrence once termed him "the gypsy cellist"), while concertmaster Raymond Gniewek prefers a drier sound. Yet I am not aware today, as I once was, of these two separate voices: each has adapted his individuality to an overall expressive flow while retaining his distinctiveness (one can usually spot a Silberstein cello solo!).

James Levine himself is extremely pleased with the sound of his orchestra. "When I came to the house, the orchestra could play several things very well: the big showpieces, like *Salome*, and the day-to-day operas, like *Tosca*. I try each year to work on one aspect of orchestral performance—chordings, balance, color—and as that becomes ingrained and naturally articulated, go on to others. I know exactly what I'll be working on with them next year.

"I'm quite pleased with the Wagner operas I've conducted, and think that in Verdi I have instilled the kind of energy I want, but not yet the flexibility I would like to have. When I came, the orchestra's Mozart playing was well behind its other playing— simply not comparable to that of the Vienna Philharmonic or several English orchestras in terms of color, inflection, and line. They don't yet have it in their blood, as those others do. But I felt that with this year's *Così* we were at least in the ballpark, and we should do better in next year's *Idomeneo*.

"One beneficial result of last year's strike has been the addition of a pool of rotating orchestra players. Because of this, I have had to go over the basics again with everybody, and this has had good results."

Violinist Toni Rapport began playing at the Met in 1968, and she too feels that there is a great difference in the orchestral playing.

"This orchestra is a symphony orchestra that plays opera," she said. "And I can't tell you how much I have learned since I came here."

Rapport feels strongly that the four-performance-a-week contract won by the orchestra in the labor dispute has had an effect, on morale and on playing.

"For me, it is an enormous difference. Before, there was a feeling of drudgery brought on by physical exhaustion, but now, even though we have the same number of rehearsals, that one performance fewer clears my mind and gives me a fresher outlook."

Since Rapport has three children and a full home life, the extra evening off has meant more to her than to those without families. "I get to see more of my family and friends, and I even get to go out occasionally. I've even come to the Met as a member of the audience. I can't tell you how different it is to hear a performance from the auditorium than in the pit. You get a completely separate perspective."

Rapport, who, like Ouzounian, is an opera lover, claims that her violin playing has been influenced by the singing she hears, "particularly Leontyne Price's phrasing in the Verdi Requiem." (Ouzounian, however, cautions on judging singers from the pit, without seeing them: he said he could never understand why Jon Vickers's Otello was so well received until he saw his performance on television.)

There is no question that Levine's insistence on getting the orchestra onstage for several performances each year (as with the Verdi Requiem) has affected morale. Even the most hardened *routinier* cannot help being infected by the enthusiasm surrounding such an event.

Two points should be made with respect to the improvement in the orchestra. The first is that if this orchestra is as good as its supporters believe it to be, it should not be confined to the conductors, aside from Levine, who direct it night after night. Great symphony orchestras—Berlin, Chicago, Boston, Philadelphia— become sounding boards for the talents of major conductors of the world, all of whom bring differing concepts to the music played. The complexities surrounding opera versus symphonic performance are well-known and admitted; but even so, is it finally worth building up a group of this talent and then not going the extra lengths to persuade major conductors to work with it? Cannot a major conductor be given a single program, like the Verdi Requiem or the two Sunday concerts scheduled this year? It might mean extra expense to schedule a total of four performances over a two-week span, in order to tempt someone to come to the Met, but that expense is artistically justified. If Levine can turn over his operas to Angelo Campori and Thomas Fulton, as he did this year, certainly someone else could take over the last two or three performances for a guest conductor, to make a respectable run of six or seven. Levine once said that he had proposed to Karajan the idea of bringing over his production of *Salome* from Salzburg and having Levine, as music director, rehearse it, so that Karajan would only have to arrive for the dress rehearsal. Shouldn't this be part of the task of the music director of a major opera house? And what about co-producing opera productions, as Los Angeles and Covent Garden did in 1982 with Verdi's *Falstaff* in order to lure Carlo Maria Giulini back into the opera pit? It is always easier to say "no" than to dare.

The second point is deflationary. Opera orchestras, no matter how good they are, are only opera orchestras. If their playing (with a few operatic exceptions, and Beecham's exhortation "Louder—I can still hear the singers!" to the contrary notwithstanding) is supreme, it is still meant as accompaniment to the singers and to the drama onstage; and to the extent that the orchestra arrogates the primary role, it is upsetting the natural balance of opera. Very few in the audience pay fifty dollars and downwards to hear the Met orchestra, even with Levine.

And yet, even with that said, it is evident that the vitality and accomplishment of the orchestra is the brightest area of improvement at the Met—brighter than the stagings, the consistency of night-to-night performance, the work of the supporting singers and chorus, and even brighter than the house's attempts to introduce twentieth-century works. One can hear something becoming better year by year, in a way not comparable to whatever progress is being made onstage. I often find myself shutting my eyes and listening to the orchestra—unthinkable a few years ago. Perhaps that is because there is a music director; perhaps it is because of the lack of great singers and—more appropriately—great singing. At all events, it is a fact—or as Gertrude Stein put it in the final words of *Four Saints in Three Acts*: "WHICH IS A FACT."

M A R C H

22	23	24	25	26	27	27
Die Entführung aus dem Serail	**I vespri siciliani**	**Les Contes d'Hoffmann**	**Il barbiere di Siviglia**	**Die Entführung aus dem Serail**	**Les Contes d'Hoffmann**	**I vespri siciliani**
Levine;	*Levine;*	*Chailly;*	*Davis;*	*Levine;*	*Chailly;*	*Levine;*
Moser,	*Scotto,*	*Welting,*	*Battle,*	*Moser,*	*Welting,*	*Scotto,*
Battle,	*Ochman,*	*Eda-Pierre,*	*Blake,*	*Battle,*	*Eda-Pierre,*	*Ochman,*
Burrows,	*Elvira,*	*Troyanos,*	*Workman,*	*Burrows,*	*Troyanos,*	*Elvira,*
Creech,	*Raimondi*	*Howells,*	*Capecchi,*	*Creech,*	*Howells,*	*Raimondi*
Talvela		*Domingo,*	*Montarsolo*	*Talvela*	*Domingo,*	
		Morris			*Morris*	

The National Council
and the Auditions

The National Council of the Metropolitan Opera held the finals of its National Auditions on the stage of the Met on Sunday afternoon, March 21, at two o'clock. This event has long been a fixture, and is one way in which the Met aspires to be a national opera company not only in the works it presents and the stars it showcases, but in the development of future talent.

The National Council of the Metropolitan Opera was founded by Mrs. August Belmont in 1952 to extend the reach of the Met beyond that served by the Opera Guild, and beyond the modest financial reach of the Guild's national members. It was from the beginning coordinated with the Met's annual tour, but it included regions not covered by those performances.

The National Council has always been a small organization of people in various cities who wish to participate in some way in the Met's activities. The National Council holds two meetings each opera season in New York, one in the autumn and one in the spring, when there is a plethora of partying as well as a steady diet of Met performances.

The National Council, whose president is Mrs. Gilbert W. Humphrey of Cleveland, numbers over seven hundred, and its contributions to the Met come more from the fact that its members are patrons than through the organization itself.

To outsiders, the National Council has always appeared to be a group of the moneyed who like an excuse for getting together, but this view seriously underestimates the work the Council has accomplished for opera over the years.

There are two main constituents to the National Council's work: the Central Opera Service and the National Auditions Program.

The Central Opera Service, run for years by the invaluable Maria F. Rich, acts as a clearinghouse for opera and sponsors various regional conferences (and an annual national conference) on aspects of opera. The national conference in 1981, held in St. Louis, concentrated on regional companies; the 1982 conference, in Miami, on "concepts and styles of operatic stage direction." Transcripts of the conferences are published in the COS's quarterly *Bulletin*, a chockablock publication intended as "a guide for opera administrators, boards of directors, trustees, and volunteers," and which includes not only what seems like every item of news about opera in the United States and Canada, but a great deal besides.

For years, the *Bulletin* has published the United States Opera Survey (which is extrapolated yearly in *Opera News*): a listing of the opera companies (large, small, college, and workshop), number of performances (standard repertory, contemporary foreign and American, and musicals), number of operas, premieres, and audiences.

In 1980–81, for instance, there were a total of 1,019 groups who gave 9,683 performances of 559 operas, plus 2,251 performances of 118 musicals—including 88 world premieres—to an audience of over eleven million at an expense of over two hundred million dollars. (Contrast this with, say, 1970–71, a decade before, when 685 companies gave 5,246 performances of 324 operas [35 world premieres] to an audience of six million.)

The COS *Bulletin*—one of a number of COS publications—contains a host of additional data: sets and costumes for rent or sale; new English translations of operas; lists of contemporary American operas (with length, cast requirements, and publisher). It has provided and continues to provide a resource not only for those in opera administration, but for all who are interested in opera, as well as a central source that documents the vitality of the art form throughout the United States.

The other arm of the National Council is the National Auditions Program. In fact, the auditions themselves antedated the creation of the National Council, for they began in 1935 and included among early winners Leonard Warren (co-winner of the third auditions).

The Auditions Program is among the widest known of all Met endeavors, simply because as a nationwide talent hunt it comes to the attention of newspapers and radio stations around the country from Hawaii to Maine. There are other singers' audition programs (notably the Merola Auditions of the San Francisco Opera), but the net the Met auditions casts is encompassing, and the notable graduates of the program—both winners and also-rans—have stocked opera houses for over forty years.

The National Auditions Program, today under the direction of former Met mezzo-soprano Risë Stevens, is a pyramidal structure, beginning at the grass roots with district regional auditions throughout the United States and even elsewhere, regional auditions finals, leading up to the audition semifinals in New York (onstage at the Met), followed, a week later, by the finals, again onstage, and this time before an audience.

The format of the National Auditions has recently been changed. At one time, the finals were part of the competition, in that prizes were awarded for the first three places, and for several years the winner was given a Met contract. This was never entirely satisfactory, for the Met's representatives often chose winners more because of their own needs than on an evaluation of the best voice or the one with the most promise. Moreover, Met officials were rarely happy with the professionality of the finalists, who were, after all, only beginning their careers. Only once or twice in a decade does a Leonard Warren emerge.

Now, however, the competition as such ends with the choice of the finalists. All finalists receive study grants of five thousand dollars each, and the finals program itself is considered less a competition than a showcase, for the public and for directors of opera companies or their representatives.

Stevens maintains that the new format has several advantages. It means that the finalists can prepare their selections (with the Met staff, particularly coach Joan Dornemann and language coach Nico Castel) with a greater ease and confidence, and that the atmosphere during that finals week (which includes appearances on radio) is one of camaraderie rather than competition. The format also allows for performance of duets, which can be of value in determining musicianship in ensemble work and voice blending in performance, two considerations not readily audible from solo selections. (All finalists sing a solo selection as well.)

In 1982, there were twenty-two semifinalists and eleven finalists, chosen from fifteen hundred singers heard in the United States, Canada, Puerto Rico, Mexico, and Australia. Stevens stated, in her speech to the audience at the finals, that the requirements for judgment were a voice of exceptional quality, musicianship, and "that special magic" which transforms a singer into an opera performer.

The National Auditions Program, no less than any other of the Met's programs, assiduously pursues underwriting. Numerous individuals donate funds for prizes, along with corporations and foundations; this year Warner Communications made a three-year pledge of $450,000 to the Young Artists Program ($50,000 a year of it as a challenge), and this was announced during the auditions finals.

The auditions finals may no longer have their edge of "Who is going to win?"; but they are still a lively event, adroitly stage managed and professionally run. The Met's stage was decorated by the Act II, scene 2 set of *La traviata*, without gambling table and without the aura of an upper-class house of assignation, and with a grand piano added. The speeches were short (Howard Hook, longtime chairman of the Auditions Program, was given the National Council's Verdi Medal of Achievement). The winners sang twenty numbers, which included an eyebrow-raising total of eight from French operas (Castel must have been kept busy during the week teaching French diction!), six from Italian, one from German (Richard Strauss), and five from Mozart (in Italian and German).

As always, audience members disagreed with each other about the merits and demerits of the singers (as did those backstage), although there was general agreement that one of the sopranos, Hei Kyung Hong (from Korea by way of New Jersey) was more polished and poised than the rest—as well she should have been: she had come from singing to acclaim at the Juilliard School an extremely demanding role in Roger Sessions's difficult *Montezuma*, and had appeared as Mimi on Korean National Television.

Standards of judgment, however, must be different from those used for professional performance. What is looked for is potential as much as finish, and what is looked for especially is the glimmer of a voice of special qualities—size, drama, lyricism, agility. This year, oddly, produced no basses or baritones as finalists (especially odd since the lyric baritone is an American specialty), but that was in part ascribed to the general lack of male operatic voices (as opposed to the plethora of female).

If the Met no longer gives contracts for in-house performances to winners, it retains the right to invite those whom it likes to become part of its Young Artist Development Program. The Young Artist Program is the Met's present-day equivalent of the earlier Metropolitan Opera Studio. It is, however, run differently. The aim is to give certain singers time to work on their voices, on their stage deportment, and with languages; and to that end they are given two-year contracts, with an option (on the Met's part) for a third. In return, the Met has a veto power over the singers' outside engagements, if the management feels that the role offered is not right for the developing voice. In fact, the veto is often a consultative decision between the singer and either Met assistant artistic administrator Lawrence Stayer (in charge of the program) or Joan Ingpen or James Levine, for the Met very much wants the singers to accept outside work (since they do not appear at first in any Met productions) and, indeed, assists in their preparation of outside roles. The young American baritone Brian Schexnayder, for instance, was asked to sing the demanding role of Gerard in Giordano's *Andrea Chenier*. He felt he was ready to undertake it for the few performances scheduled, and so did Stayer: Schexnayder now will work on it with the Met's staff. In the 1982–83 season, moreover, Schexnayder is to appear at the Met as Enrico (opposite Joan Sutherland) in *Lucia di Lammermoor*.

There are currently ten singers in the Young Artist Program; and after some initial reluctance on the part of young singers, who were justifiably wary that the Met was trying to develop not future stars but a complaisant cadre of comprimario artists, the program has become popular enough so that the Met now holds periodic auditions for those wishing to join. So far, however, the members of the program have come not through auditions of this sort, but through the National Auditions Program and through referrals by voice teachers, singers, or those in the Met management.

Joan Ingpen is rightly worried about the singers' future after their two or three years are finished. If the Met feels that further schooling is necessary, she and her colleagues will try to develop a longer-based program of roles in the house, which the singer is free to accept or reject. Along with many of her colleagues, Ingpen is aware of the dangers of young singers overusing their voices and coming to early ruin; yet there is a fine line between continued healthy development and treading water, which each singer must ultimately answer for himself or herself.

Several young singers were brought in by the current management before the Young Artist Program was created. One of these is Timothy Jenkins, who was "discovered" by Ingpen.

Jenkins, born in Amarillo, Texas, studied voice at the music school of North Texas State University—one of the largest music schools in the country, and one with a fine reputation—and entered the Met regional auditions in New Orleans as a baritone. He was not a finalist, but Ingpen, who was one of the judges, was impressed by the size and the potential of his voice and asked him whether he had ever thought of becoming a tenor—or, more specifically, a Heldentenor, or Wagnerian tenor.

Heldentenors are ever at a premium. The classic example of Lauritz Melchior, the greatest Wagnerian tenor of this century, is that of a baritone converted upward; and this has been the route thought most promising for that breed, although two notable twentieth-century Heldentenors, Max Lorenz and Wolfgang Windgassen, began singing as tenors.

Ingpen's suggestion met with Jenkins's and his voice teacher's approval, and Jenkins was brought to the Met under contract.

"If it had not been for Miss Ingpen, I would not have had the money to spend the years necessary to convert to tenor, and I probably would have continued as a Verdi baritone, accepting whatever was offered."

The process of conversion can be a lengthy one, and too early singing of demanding tenor parts can ruin the voice and leave the singer crippled both as a baritone and as a tenor.

Since coming to the Met, Jenkins has put himself entirely in the hands of Ingpen and James Levine. He has no manager, and consults with Ingpen as to offers he receives. Since his voice is remarkable, such offers have already been made—Ingpen turned down one for a major Wagnerian tenor role from the Bavarian Radio.

In 1981–82 he cautiously sang a few low tenor parts (such as the Armed Man in *Zauberflöte*, once sung at the Met by James McCracken); but he is not overworked. "I feel it is a blessing to have the opportunity to develop as a singer at one's own pace in this house. It's a healthy environment, and I know I'm not being exploited. I have the final say as to not doing roles assigned me. If I think it's too much, I tell Miss Ingpen."

Jenkins feels he is, at present, vocally ready to take on bigger tenor roles. His schedule for 1982–83 is much larger: he is to appear in all three new productions (*Arabella*, *Idomeneo*, and *Macbeth*) and in addition is to take on the demanding role of Parsifal.

Parsifal, in fact, is one of the least demanding of major Wagner tenor roles—about a half hour of singing, concentrated in the second act, and not lying high for the voice. And Jenkins will have the further advantage of going to Bayreuth in the summer of 1982 to work with Levine while the conductor prepares the centennial production of *Parsifal* there.

Whether Timothy Jenkins will develop into a Heldentenor of consequence is for the future. But to the Met management the financial gamble is well worth it. And Ingpen feels that the way in which Jenkins's career has been handled, in his change from baritone to tenor, enhances the chances for his future success.

29	30	31	1	2	3	3
Fidelio	**Les Contes**	**Die**	**I vespri**	**Fidelio**	**Die**	**Les Contes**
Haitink;	**d'Hoffmann**	**Entführung**	**siciliani**	*Haitink;*	**Entführung**	**d'Hoffmann**
Verrett,	*Chailly;*	**aus dem**	*Levine;*	*Meier,*	**aus dem**	*Chailly;*
Blegen,	*Welting,*	**Serail**	*Scotto,*	*Blegen,*	**Serail**	*Welting,*
Sooter,	*Eda-Pierre,*	*Levine;*	*Moldoveanu,*	*Sooter,*	*Levine;*	*Eda-Pierre,*
Roar,	*V. Cortez,*	*Devia,*	*Elvira,*	*Roar,*	*Devia,*	*V. Cortez,*
Macurdy	*Howells,*	*Battle,*	*Raimondi*	*Macurdy*	*Battle,*	*Howells,*
	Domingo,	*Burrows,*			*Burrows,*	*Domingo,*
	Morris	*Atherton,*			*Creech,*	*Morris*
		Talvela/			*Talvela/*	
		Berberian			*Berberian*	

Fund Raising

In order that there be an artistic product at the Metropolitan Opera, there has to be a fund-raising effort: constant, incessant, and ever-expanding. The Met, as an institution given to charitable deduction of contributions but only minorly given state and federal arts subsidies, has always trod the path between solvency and bankruptcy. The 1920s were years in which the company made money; the early 1930s were years in which it almost went out of business. And the same process was repeated after the Second World War, particularly after the move to Lincoln Center in 1966.

Opera the way the Met believes in doing it is fearsomely expensive, and it is presented in a building that is fearsomely expensive to maintain. That building, moreover, is sixteen years old, and already in need of refurbishing before and behind the gold curtain (to the tune of at least $2 million). The built-in cost, which increases from year to year, by union contract and by inflation, cannot be matched by raising ticket prices; thus, each year, a larger sum must be garnered by fund appeals to contributors: from $10 million to $12 million to $14 million to, now, $18.1 million.*

It is not difficult to understand why more than a few Met board members became discouraged in the late 1960s and early 1970s when presented with extrapolations of future money raising. Some felt that such a continuing and ever-growing task was impossible and that the Met faced several hard choices: to reorganize on a smaller, more limited basis for a short annual season; to bring in a ballet company to share the burden (but which one would accept?); to "get rid" of the costly building to Lincoln Center (but would Lincoln Center accept it?); or, at worst, to give up and go out of business as a casualty of inflation and the peripheral artistic value of opera in twentieth-century American society.

These questions all had to be addressed in the severe fiscal crisis of 1977. And the decision taken was none of the above. Because of the strong advocacy of then–general manager Schuyler Chapin, and the equally strong backing of his eventual successor, Anthony Bliss, it was decided to continue as before, effecting every economy possible but not compromising artistic quality, and to go out and find the money necessary. Today, because of the steady and unflinching guidance of Bliss and the Met's working board president Frank Taplin, the Met stands, if not secure, at least on a far sounder financial ground than at any time in the recent past; and there is an optimism backstage and, significantly, on the board level that was not present six years ago.

This relative security has been attained through a combination of ruthless professionalization of the fund-raising apparatus, constant explorations of every avenue that might lead to monies, and early and perceptive realization by Bliss and the board that federal and state subsidies could not be relied on for significant ongoing funds. This demanded involvement of Met board members as

---

*This figure was accurate for 1981–82 at the time of writing. By fall 1982, however, it was close to $18.9 million.

active, unpaid fund raisers the year around. Indeed, the inventiveness of the Met in capturing every loose dollar rivals its inventiveness and expertise onstage, and it is not too farfetched to state that as a fund raiser the Met is even more professionally adept than the singers and conductors it presents as end products.

Anthony Bliss, in 1981 named general manager, and Frank Taplin, a beaver of activity for the company, are the two most prominent figures in that money search. But the instigation and coordination of most of the fund activities lie in the hands and brain of assistant manager Marilyn Shapiro.

Shapiro was brought to the Met for her knowledge of the Washington bureaucratic scene (she had been administrative assistant to former New York City congresswoman Elizabeth Holtzman), to help out with federal grants; but when it soon became apparent that the Met's salvation did not lie in that direction, Shapiro shifted her focus to fund raising, a job that consumes all her time.

Shapiro is a dilly of a fund raiser. An intense, voluble woman who confesses to being an opera buff ("but operas with tunes"—although she doesn't want that enthusiasm emphasized), she sees her job as that of Sisyphus rolling the stone.

"Every year we go back to square one, except that the amount to be raised increases. In the spring, I make up a budget of what I realistically think I can raise in the coming year. The house then gives me a figure of what they think, based on the repertory, new productions and whatever, they need. Then we negotiate. My bottom-line number is fairly conservative: this year the figure is 18.1 million to be raised, and in September I was reasonably sure I could come up with 17.3 million of it. By mid-winter I was reasonably sure of 17.9, and now I think we'll just about make it. But next year it will be more."

Some of this money is reliable: funds supplied by the Opera Guild members, the patrons, and the radio donors.

"I have never believed that there is a finite amount of money out there which we cannot top. If I believed that, I wouldn't be in this job. I'm an optimist: the glass is always half full for me."

One of the major vexations of fund raising is the "windfall," or one-shot, nature of much of it. Neither the government, nor foundations, nor corporations will grant ongoing, steady support, which is of course vital. All of them prefer to fund special projects (which give them publicity visibility), which may in time be completed or which may suddenly be terminated with changes in corporate or foundation management or changes in government thinking. This year, for instance, Merrill, Lynch has made a grant of $300,000 toward the Met tour. The Met, naturally, would like to count on its continuation, and even its augmentation, in future years, but it cannot. If someone dies and leaves the Met a million dollars, that alleviates the financial burden in the year the money is received, but not in the next.

It is because of the unevenness of the Met's support, which cannot be counted on or budgeted, and because of the constantly rising amount to be raised, that the Met (at Frank Taplin's instigation) began its Centennial Fund campaign, to raise $100 million ($1 million for every year the Met has been in existence) to act as an endowment fund. When the money is in place, this fund will be able to manipulate its portfolio of investments so that it can generate more income in years when that is needed and more growth when that is indicated.

The national chairman of the Centennial Fund is John K. McKinley, who happens to be the chairman and chief executive officer of the Met's longtime sponsor Texaco—and who also, luckily, happens to be an opera buff. He, Taplin, David M. Roderick (chairman of the board and chief executive officer of U.S. Steel), who is national corporate chairman, and others have tapped corporate and private foundations all over the United States to raise (by 1982) almost $60 million, of which $20 million is in hand.

The Met is careful, however, to insist that even if the $100 million is raised, it will not and cannot take the place of the annual appeals. The fund can act only as a safety net; and by the terms under which it is set up, the board cannot invade its capital except in dire emergencies—and then only the unrestricted funds.

Yet the existence of the fund, the existence of more or less regular contributions from a variety of members of Met support organizations, and the ongoing and relentless search for dollars have generated a climate of financial stability. The annual "emergency appeal" of so many yesteryears had in time achieved a diminishing effect, for the Met can cry wolf only so often before donors—and particularly foundations—will choose to take their money elsewhere, feeling that it is useless to pour money down a bottomless well. It may be paradoxical, but all professional fund raisers agree that the healthier an organization is in terms of fund raising, balance sheets, and morale, the more money it can raise. People naturally want to be with a winner. Thus, even though the 1980–81 season was curtailed by the lockout and the bitterness that followed it, annual giving held up.

"The Met family stood by us," Shapiro said. "After all, opera does generate passion. It's a special art form, and an emotional turn-on like no other."

The concept of the Met family, as has been said before, is integral to all Met fund raising. The Met goes to great lengths to please its donors, commensurate with the amounts they give. Since the yearly goal, for instance, is to increase the number of patrons by two hundred—which means adding more than that number, since there are always some patrons who don't renew—everyone must work at it, from the in-house staff to the members of the board.

"It's safe to say," said public relations director David Reuben, "that somewhere in New York, every week in the winter, there's a party for the patrons."

Patrons were invited to the kickoff fund raiser on the stage of the Met the night before opening (the Met Marathon), which was broadcast nationwide. Later in the year, higher-category patrons (five thousand dollars and up) were invited to a seated dinner on the stage of the Met, replete with caviar and free-flowing champagne (courtesy of the management), surrounded by some of David Hockney's designs, and attended by a variety of roster artists, not least James Levine himself. When board members give parties for patrons in their apartments, there are always singers in attendance.

The management is constantly at work devising new opportunities for giving. The Fund for Productions raises money for new productions and revivals; the Golden Horseshoe requires a major financial commitment over a three-year span, in return for which the contributor's name is put on a plaque in the house and is cited in the evening's program at the bottom of the cast list: "The Metropolitan Opera Association is pleased to honor —— at this evening's performance for his/her generous participation in the Golden Horseshoe." Deferred giving plans are detailed; a pamphlet entitled "The Will to Let One of the Joys of Your Life Live On and On" is sent out, describing methods of leaving bequests, gifts of jewelry, art works, antiques, and real estate. In March 1982, the Opera Guild sent out an appeal for funds to underwrite the telecasts of the two concerts (Domingo/Troyanos and Price/ Horne) given during the season—Guild members previously underwrote the *Elektra* telecast featuring Birgit Nilsson. Marilyn Shapiro and her staff are working on an idea for a Centennial Book of Names of donors to the Centennial Fund, to be kept in some appropriate place in the house.

In late February, the subscription letters and announcements of the next season's schedule were put in the mail, followed by flyers in each night's program detailing subscription opportunities for 1982–83. A table was set up on the Grand Tier level to sign up new subscribers. After the 1981–82 season ended, the Met began a five-night-a-week "phonothon" from banks of telephones set up in the Met to a list of names across the country. These calls were preceded by letters to each of the persons called, from Bliss and then from Taplin. According to Taplin, this solicitation has resulted in pledges of money from 26 percent of those called (a benchmark "good" response would be 15 percent).

This sense of family, which has been abetted by music director James Levine's ubiquitousness and seeming approachability, has transformed the once austere Met. Of the sixteen hundred patrons, seven hundred are also subscribers, and they are, in Shapiro's words, "not jet-setters but people who genuinely love opera."

Yet while producing a cohesive group who accept such artistic inevitabilities as cancellations, substitutions, and even periodic contract disputes with relative equanimity, this sense of family also produces complacency. The Met family likes what it is given, and will permit a few novelties; but it will not tolerate for long any adventurousness—either difficult operas or outré productions. The innate tendency toward the repetition of the core repertory in "Met type" productions is therefore a constant pressure: one that the management can rationalize as giving the audience the product it wants while continuing to perform the "great operas of the past." Yet too often areas of operatic history are not being explored, or explored only tentatively, with the Met insulating itself from many possible choices of noncore operas. It is indicative that to those backstage and in management, John Dexter's greatest contribution as director of productions lay not in the stagings of the operas he supervised but in his overhaul of the production facilities of the Met, putting them on a stronger organizational and financial footing.

And although the Met has opened itself to more than the elite who made up its major support in the early days, it has also, in its zeal for the big monies, tended to ignore the smaller donor. These donors had been brought into the Met family at an earlier time through Mrs. Belmont's Opera Guild; they were given free dress rehearsals, an annual event, *Opera News*, and—not inconsequentially—a sense of participation. Today, as the number of Guild members has grown, fewer are able to get into the dress rehearsals that are scheduled, there is no longer an annual event, and the parties and such are reserved for the major donors.

All of these developments in fund raising, moreover, have been so widely publicized—as they must be—that they appear to dominate all Met activities, leading inevitably to the charge that the financial tail is wagging the artistic dog. Marilyn Shapiro (quite naturally, given her job) disagrees, and she makes the following point:

"I don't see how we can be accused of controlling the artistic side, except in a general way. Joan Ingpen, Tony Bliss, and Jimmy Levine are currently planning the 1985–86 season. There is no budget for that season, and although they are putting together a mix of new productions and revivals, of appearances of the twelve or fifteen major singers the Met should have, the specific financial cost cannot be arrived at. They have to operate on the basis of the artistic, with the financial coming in at a later stage."

Yet the financial must eventually enter. Joe Volpe, the assistant manager who acts as liaison between the "front of the house" and the "back of the house" (where he began years ago as technical director and then worked as operations director), envisions a situation within the next two years when the costs of a season can be estimated, with some accuracy, a season or more ahead.

"It's a matter of programming a computer with the facts we already know about the costs of putting on a specific revival— *Tosca*, say—as to rehearsal time, onstage time, et cetera (and this depends on how long it has been out of the repertory), and adding the costs of singers, the estimated costs of new productions, with rehearsals and such, and a built-in factor for inflation. Given what we know and what we can reasonably project, we can arrive at a ballpark figure for that season. And then we can focus on what needs to be trimmed."

A P R I L

5	6	7	8	9	10	10
Parsifal	**Fidelio**	**I vespri siciliani**	**Die Entführung aus dem Serail**	**Parsifal**	**Fidelio**	**I vespri siciliani**
Levine;	*Haitink;*	*Levine;*	*Levine;*	*Levine;*	*Haitink;*	*Fulton;*
Dunn,	*Verrett,*	*Scotto,*	*Devia,*	*Dunn,*	*Meier,*	*Scotto,*
Hofmann,	*Blegen,*	*Moldoveanu,*	*Bradley,*	*Hofmann,*	*Blegen,*	*Moldoveanu,*
Stewart,	*Sooter,*	*Elvira,*	*Alexander,*	*Stewart,*	*Sooter,*	*Elvira,*
Hines,	*Roar,*	*Raimondi*	*Creech,*	*Hines,*	*Roar,*	*Furlanetto*
Meredith	*Macurdy*		*Berberian*	*Meredith*	*Macurdy*	

The Boards of Directors

Т he Metropolitan Opera Association is known by its general manager and by its singers and, in this regime, by its music director; but it is overseen by its board of directors—or, more accurately, by its boards. The smaller the board, the more important its function. Technically, the more than one hundred and forty members of the association elect the boards over them; but this body, which meets but twice a year, performs a purely legalistic role.

Above the members of the association is a bifurcated (in practice, though trifurcated in fact) board, restructured several years ago for greater efficiency. There are honorary directors selected from board members now retired from Met service. Then there are advisory directors, almost fifty in number, who meet four or five times a year with the managing directors, who number thirty. The managing directors meet once a month.

Yet, as is apparent in any large corporation, even thirty is a sizable number to oversee, discuss, and agree on the many topics that come before them. Thus, it is the executive committee of the board, a group of twelve who meet every two weeks, in whom the real board power resides; and its members are, with the addition of several others from the managing board, the most active.

The managing directors, and the executive committee drawn from them, have over the past years been shaped into a generative force to oversee the company and to raise, and keep raising, monies. They are all at least interested in opera—most have a passionate interest in it—but beyond that interest they satisfy the chief prerequisite of board members of charitable organizations: the ability either to give money or to get it. (An exception would be Wilbur Daniels, a labor executive with the Amalgamated Clothing Workers Union, who was enlisted for his contacts and expertise in the labor field and who, in the past year, has regularly met with union committees backstage as liaison between them and the board.) Those members who cannot afford to give new productions or make generous annual gifts (five to six figures are preferred) work in other ways, raising monies through developing sources of revenue, enlisting new patrons, or hosting parties. Most members of the upper board devote a significant amount of their time to the Met; in this the Met has a working board unlike some organizations, in which either the appointed head or the chief executive officer runs the show unhindered, except for rubber-stamp approval. (I remember Carol Fox of the Chicago Lyric Opera once saying to me, "Don't go to my board—I tell them what they need to know.")

There is one area that the management has tried to keep away from board control: the artistic. Several board members know a great deal about opera, and might make effective impresarios; several more know less than they think they do. But neither Rudolf Bing nor his successors have wanted interference on their artistic prerogatives. For instance, the production committee of the board, which meets irregularly, has only an advisory capacity.

It is true, though, that by virtue of its control of the finances the board does in effect have an artistic impact. Since the executive committee discusses artists' fees* and production costs, it can to an extent control what is put on; but this control is evidenced in the area of day-to-day cost control rather than the forced hiring of singer X or Y or the playing of opera Z. In the past few years, a way-over-budget new production or two has been scrapped or severely curtailed in the planning stages because of board pressure. (Ponnelle's *Aida* is one example.) The board, of course, also deals with many areas outside of main-stage activities, but which are an integral part of the Met: the annual tour, the use of the house when the company is not in residence, the purchase of the huge New Jersey warehouse, the amalgamation of Met support organizations within the house, and the ticklish and often acerbic relationship between the Met and Lincoln Center.

Anthony Bliss, as general manager, is in the curious position of having been on both sides of the management fence at the Met, and he uses that position to advantage. He has generally not interfered in artistic matters (in this respect differing from all previous general managers), allowing these to develop from his music director, James Levine, and his assistant manager, Joan Ingpen (and earlier, also from John Dexter). He has the final say, but he will not necessarily veto what has been suggested except on financial grounds. Outside the house Bliss is seen as primarily a money man, and he is content with that perception, although he does not relish being thought of, as some opera buffs do, as a person interested more in ballet than in opera.

Besides his activities as general manager, Bliss was directly responsible for having the Met take over the programs in the opera house for the period after the company goes on tour (roughly, mid-April till the end of July). These events, mostly ballet, are not contracted out to Lincoln Center or to an outside impresario.

---

*Artists' fees are one subject of inordinate interest to operagoers. The Met insists on maintaining a "top" fee, which it will not exceed, and which is less than that given by other companies here and abroad. Yet certain events, such as the concerts, are not subject to this ceiling; and, in addition, the Met has long relied on its name and renown, its TV and radio performances, to lure singers with the promotional advantages it offers them, both in the United States and beyond.

Though the Met stands to gain financially to a greater extent than it would if these attractions were contracted out, it also stands to lose if the attractions do poorly. Bliss very much believes in having the Met control its non-Met programs, which are offered first to Met subscribers and patrons, because he believes that today's arts patron wants more than simply opera. And he is enthusiastic about the abilities of his presentations director, Jane Hermann, who is in direct charge of these weeks.

William Rockefeller holds the largely ceremonial but nonetheless time-consuming job of chairman of the board (he represented the board at the Opera Ball), while Frank Taplin, who as president of the managing board is chief executive officer of the company, has what could be termed an analogous role to Bliss's, but on the board level. In the financial crisis of the spring of 1977, Taplin was brought in as a working president in order to raise funds. He had retired from business some time before, and agreed to devote three days of the week in the house (where he has a small office) to the Met.

The various committees of the managing board also provide impetus on a continuing basis. James S. Marcus, Chairman of the Executive Committee, is a particularly knowledgeable and informed board member. Executive board member (and vice-president) Bruce Crawford, who is otherwise chief executive officer of the advertising firm BBD&O, is in charge of developing the Met's programs vis-à-vis the emerging world of cable television and videodiscs and videotapes. The PBS appearances of the Met have been major audience generators and have maintained the company's national image, but they were never intended as revenue generators except in an ancillary way. Crawford is realistic in his assessment that monies from cable television and the videodisc/tape market are still some way off in the future, and will never be a panacea; but he is determined that the Met be ready when the time does arrive. To that end, the company has already videotaped over twenty performances, half of them in digital sound, and has signed a contract with the unions, after months of negotiations, for release rights and royalty payments.

The members of the managing board and their spouses see a

great deal of each other during the season, both at board meetings and at various Met events, and many of them have become friends outside the Met, linked by their love of opera. (They can be just as opinionated and contentious as standee opera buffs, and share with the standees a devotion to the opera company.) General opinion on the board as to the future is positive, from guarded optimism to outright assertions that the Centennial Fund not only will be reached but will be exceeded.

Yet there are also, of course, a few nay sayers. One board member says, "This company may not demand singers with voices, but the opera house does." He feels extremely dubious about the long-run survival of the Met in its present form, with the growing amounts to be raised, and says, "Before, the orchestra members and workers backstage bore the brunt of the opera house because they were underpaid. Now it's the patrons who are bearing the brunt." He wants the opera company thoroughly reorganized, reducing the season to November-to-April—no tour—and making every effort to get itself out of the running of the opera house, but making a comparable effort to find a smaller house for smaller-scale operas.

There is no doubt that the hierarchy now operating at the Met of Taplin as chief executive officer and Bliss as a financially oriented general manager is somewhat curious, in that it defers direct generative artistic policy to a lower level. Yet it is one that was dictated by the necessities of the time, ameliorated by the dynamic force of the ideas of Levine and Ingpen and by the willingness of both Bliss and Taplin, and through them the board, to accept those ideas as long as they were financially (rather than artistically) feasible.

APRIL

12	13	14	15	16	17	17
Die Entführung aus dem Serail	**Parsifal**	**Fidelio**	**I vespri siciliani**	**Die Entführung aus dem Serail**	**Parsifal**	**Fidelio**
Levine;	*Levine;*	*Haitink;*	*Fulton;*	*Levine;*	*Levine;*	*Haitink;*
Devia,	*Troyanos,*	*Meier,*	*Gulin,*	*Moser,*	*Dunn,*	*Verrett,*
Battle,	*Hofmann,*	*Blegen,*	*Moldoveanu,*	*Battle,*	*Hofmann,*	*Blegen,*
Burrows,	*Clark,*	*Sooter,*	*Elvira,*	*Burrows,*	*Stewart,*	*Sooter,*
Creech,	*Hines,*	*Roar,*	*Furlanetto*	*Creech,*	*Hines,*	*Roar,*
Berberian	*Meredith*	*Macurdy*		*Berberian*	*Meredith*	*Macurdy*

Finale, with Penguins

T he last week of the Met's New York season saw performances of four operas—*Die Entführung aus dem Serail, Parsifal, Fidelio,* and *I vespri siciliani*—while the backstage areas, and even the main stage, were taken over by rehearsals for the tour performances, for the new singers who would be added and for the conductors who would replace those from the season's performances. (Levine goes on the tour every other year; this year he is "off" except for two *Parsifal*s in Washington, D.C.)

It so happened that the season's final New York performance—*Fidelio* on Saturday evening, April 17—was a non-subscription one, and was the occasion of the twenty-second annual Opera Ball, an event run by the Metropolitan Opera Club.

The Metropolitan Opera Club has had a long history in the house, extending back to the company's earliest days. It began in 1893 as the Vaudeville Club, an organization devoted to light entertainment and refreshment, which leased rooms in the old house when the company had to suspend its season because of a fire onstage. When the Met resumed performances, the club contracted for a box to view the operas, and gradually the "vaudeville" aspects of the club's endeavors were phased out. It became a fully operatic adjunct to the house in 1899.

The Metropolitan Opera Club has long been the house's most conservative standard bearer of decorum, in dress at least. Black tie is obligatory for evening performances, and on the sacrosanct Mondays white tie is preferred, leading to the popular sobriquet, which the club has smilingly adopted, of "the Penguins" (a name coined, so the tale goes, by longtime Met tenor, and longtime Club member, Giovanni Martinelli).* The name arose from the sight of that phalanx of males, gathered together in the big box facing the Opera Guild box in the old opera house (though club members are now strung out over several Dress Circle boxes in the new one), which inevitably called to mind those Antarctican rookeries of *National Geographic* photographs.

The twentieth century has intruded on the club in at least one respect. Now, it is compelled to admit women as subscribing members—a few at least—though it is unlikely they will ever achieve half the membership. Club vice-president Thomas S. Brush said: "We have a dress code problem, of course, because women shouldn't come in their street clothes. But what should they wear? I suggested that they should dress in black and white, like we do, but my wife shot that one down."

Brush, who is also a managing director of the Met board, chairman of the administrative committee of the National Council, and a major donor, is an instantly recognizable figure in the opera house, with his beard, pointed mustaches, crew-cut hair, and ever-

---

*The club's rule of silence in the box was relaxed for Martinelli, who often attended performances and hummed his way through all of them. I remember one night—an *Otello* with James McCracken—when Martinelli, seated next to me, was particularly incensed. He kept saying "No, no!" and singing Otello's phrase his way, stating (correctly) that McCracken declaimed rather than sang the part and was traditionally all wrong.

present cowboy boots. That he bears a distinct resemblance to past Met general manager Giulio Gatti-Casazza has not escaped notice, either.

The club box in the old house had an advantage the new one does not. It was directly across the corridor from the Club Room, and always accessible, so that members could sit and drink and then nip over when the soprano sang her mad scene. The Club Room today, however, where pre-opera dinners are served and drinks are available during intermissions, has no such easy access: one must go to the boxes through the Dress Circle, and the doors are shut when the music begins. Various tunneling schemes from Club Room to club boxes have been explored, as yet to no avail.

The club is open on certain subscription Mondays, Wednesdays, and Fridays and on Saturday matinees (when tea is served in the Club Room), although it is extending its schedule to additional nights and would eventually like to be open every night but Saturday.

When the club instituted a junior membership at reduced rates in the old house, I was proposed for membership by my ex-pediatrician, a bachelor who had been a past club president and who spent every available evening in the opera house, often leaving in mid-performance for an emergency call. (He used to say to me, "I've slept through the best of them."*) I welcomed the chance to hear numerous operas without having to go to the trouble of buying tickets, as did my confrères, and I would have donned clown costume to do so had that been the requirement.

The club membership was, and is, a devoted band of opera lovers. One member was feted on the occasion of his one hundred and fiftieth *Tristan* (not all of them, of course, had been heard in the house), while another, who had retired in his early forties from a very successful business, kept meticulous records of every performance he heard; on Thursdays (a non-club day) he used to

---

*Another of his comments I have often used about routine repertory performances: "It needs a collective glycerine suppository up the rear."

gather musicians at his house to play string quartets. Still, since the days of Rudolf Bing, it has always been looked at askance by the management, which sees it as an anachronism. If the management has not succeeded in eliminating the club (it has, in fact, only fitfully tried to do so), it has imposed upon the club the requirement of carrying its own financial weight, as with any support organization. Today the price of appearing in black or white tie and having a private Club Room for dinners and intermissions is bought at a greater premium than before. A few years ago club members made donations toward a new gold curtain (the gold curtain is not a permanent fixture and, because of the use it sees, must be replaced every twelve years), and members are expected to support the annual Opera Ball.

The Opera Ball began, in the old house, as a social gathering which incidentally raised a few dollars for the Met. It is now Big Time, involving a season-long effort of a dedicated ball committee and numerous volunteers to raise about fifty thousand dollars. Several years ago the club hit on the excellent idea of having a foreign government sponsor the ball, thus giving its official imprimatur while pulling in contributions from various national business organizations, which buy space in the ball program and whose members buy tickets. In addition, there is a silent auction of expensive items, this year including a Renault *Fuego*. Host nation for 1982 was France, and the coat of arms of the République Française was in place on the Dress Circle railing, while the Tricolore hung over the revelers. (The choice of opera rarely coincides with the host nation, because that choice is limited to one of the few evenings that are non-subscription. This year the opera was the German national treasure *Fidelio*, but at least Beethoven and his librettists had based the opera on a French revolutionary "rescue opera," *Léonore*.)

The ball began immediately after the opera, with a seated buffet dinner (foie gras and lobster, Charolais beef, chocolate truffles, five kinds of champagnes, and fifteen red and white wines—France has certain advantages as host!), during which speeches were made, "The Marseillaise" and "The Star-Spangled Banner" were played, and Meyer Davis's orchestra, "under the baton of fellow Club member, and nephew of Pierre Monteux, Emery Davis," played incongruous Viennese waltzes and other music for the dancers. After dinner there was a *dégustation* of several cognacs, Armagnacs, and liqueurs in the Belmont Room (the fact that wine importer Peter M. F. Sichel is a club member no doubt aided this flow of the grape), star turns by two French chanteuses, and a cabaret in the Club Room which went on until dawn, when breakfast was served to those who remained.

The list of those who donated food, drink, and services to the ball filled the over-hundred-page ball program, along with articles on the club and on the Paris Opéra, plus a list of French operas and artists heard during the Met's history. The more than seven hundred people who attended the ball all seemed to be having a fine time (more white ties in evidence than on any other Met night, including opening night).

It was a particular pleasure to see among the artists there baritone Sherrill Milnes. Milnes, a reigning Met star and mainstay of the company, had canceled his engagements this winter because of a ruptured capillary in his throat, and wild rumors about his illness had swept the house for months. Singers, no less than dancers, are especially prone to illnesses that can damage and even destroy a career at its height, which is one reason why singers cannot really be faulted for oversinging in their glory years: they don't know when or if the gift will be suddenly withdrawn. George London is but one example of a career cut short by God. But Milnes is beginning to sing once more, and the sigh of relief around the Met can be heard for miles, for besides being a major baritone, Milnes is one of the nicest singers in the business.

I did not stay until dawn. Shortly after 3:00 a.m. I wended my unsteady way with my wife down the grand staircase to the cloakroom to pick up my raincoat, as it was raining lightly outside. The evening's final performance had been oddly symbolic of the season: a cast not up to the requirements of Beethoven's only opera, one of the greatest works in the core repertory, conducted in what I thought was splendid if somewhat lyric style by Bernard Haitink (others thought his conducting "too symphonic"). The orchestra sounded a mite tired, for some of them had played five hours of *Parsifal* under Levine in that afternoon's broadcast, but the players obviously respect and admire the music director of the Amsterdam Concertgebouw and the chief conductor of the Glyndebourne Opera (obviously, because more than a few of them remained behind in the orchestra pit to applaud him when he took his solo curtain—their highest accolade).

As I put on my raincoat, I looked at the portraits next to the cloakroom in Founder's Hall. Emma Eames, American soprano, 258 performances of 21 operas in the house and a further 162 on tour. Elisabeth Rethberg, German (later American) soprano, 270 performances of 30 operas in the house and 80 performances on tour; and her husband, George Cehanovsky, Russian (later American) baritone, a fixture as a comprimario with the company, singing over 2,200 times in a forty-year span.

It was as good a place as any to end the season, and to reflect on the past and the present of the repertory company known as the Metropolitan Opera.

Epilogue

It is inordinately difficult to sum up any repertory season in anything but the most obvious ways: that is, the new productions, the new singers and conductors. These give an adequate snapshot and can limn strengths and weaknesses, but they are only indications of one year out of many.

The current Met management (no less, in fact, than any previous one) claims that it views the repertory over a three- or four-year span, and James Levine prefers to talk about a run of operas and casts under his direction as conductor rather than about any single performance. He maintains that in a given season the *Don Carlo* or *Tannhäuser* or *Parsifal*—three operas that are "special projects" for him, and that he likes to keep in the Met repertory—may contain lesser singers in certain roles, for a variety of good reasons, and may not be played as well as possible, but that over the four-year span of revivals the performances will include most if not all the notable current exemplars of the leading roles and will continue to improve orchestrally and as an ensemble.

Yet it is also true that there is a gulf between what the music director performs and what other conductors perform, on a continuing basis. Continuity seems reserved for the music director: other operas are rarely given to the same conductor for two successive years.

If one can step back a few paces from the minutiae of the season, however, and go beyond the weary tales of lack of singers, problems of scheduling, and all the rest of the baggage of repertory opera, one can see a pattern that defines less the Met than the current way, worldwide, of producing opera, of which the Met is willy-nilly a part.

This is the accent on the visual. This theme has run like a ground bass through the book and represents a fundamental change in opera from the days when the singer took absolute precedence. It is seen more egregiously abroad than at the Met in terms of idiosyncratic productions, but it can be seen in various ways at the Met, too.

Today's opera audiences are more than ever before attracted by what they see rather than what they hear. The subscribers and ticket buyers may like to hear Caballé or Sutherland or Milnes or Pavarotti or Domingo, but overall they focus on the visual and not on the audible.

The Met has moved to satisfy this in several ways. One of John Dexter's values was that he was addicted to the kind of white raking light popularized by Brecht-derived stagings—the so-called "working light" used in rehearsals, which Brecht used to detheatricalize the performing event. This light may be cold and remote, as it is in the staging of *I vespri siciliani*, where it is used to suggest the Sicilian sun, and it may hurt the eyes after a while. But the audience can clearly see what is going on. Wieland Wagner's essays in chiaroscuro, carried on by Karajan and a school of 1950s and 1960s stage directors, have now been banished, at least as far as the Met is concerned. (It is notable that in the best current example of this, the aforementioned Zeffirelli lighting of Act III of *La Bohème*, the extremely effective chiaroscuro evoked the background and the supernumerary actors: the principals were kept to the front of the stage and were clearly seen.) The fact that the lights are up delights the audience, for complaints about stage darkness outweigh any other subscriber complaints.

Added to this, operatic acting has been brought closer to stage (or movie and television) acting. If the traditional overweight singer with five semaphore gestures (one for joy, one for sadness, etc.) is still on view every week, there has been a conscious effort to standardize performances in respect to the comprimarios and (insofar as possible!) the chorus. Placido Domingo's work as the drunken

Hoffmann in the Prologue and the Epilogue of *Les Contes d'Hoff-mann* demonstrated the effort he had put into the visual side of that role—an effort many tenors of his stature would not have made.

The Met goes to extreme lengths to reproduce exactly what was staged in the first performance. Its production books, six inches thick, contain precise movement directions and sheaves of contact photographs showing every step taken. To some observers, this has meant the homogenization of the product, and on several occasions I witnessed a major singer trying to fight his or her way out of the production straitjacket into a sense of individual response—perhaps at odds with the direction, and perhaps finally more superficial, but still something personal and alive. Levine maintains the contrary: that a vital production will not be affected by its standardization from one performance to the next, while a dull production will not be able to be rescued. To an extent (as discussed in "The Orchestra"), each performance creates anew, as it must; but each performance today is under more control than ever before.

But the visual extends beyond this quality control, beyond the fact that the stage can be seen. It extends, in one direction, to the artistry of the stage picture. There are sharp differences of opinion about the designs of David Hockney and of Hayden Griffin (who set *Cosi*) or of Robin Wagner (who set *Barbiere*); but the general impression is that there has been a continuing attention paid to the artistic side of the visual, which has gone far beyond the old-fashioned painted flats of yesteryear. There seems an awareness on the part of management that its audience is more broadly artistically oriented than heretofore and will appreciate color harmonies and styles of visual sophistication beyond what was once the norm. Certainly Met audiences are more than ever before frequenters of art galleries and museums and are at least tangentially aware of developments in the art world. The state-of-the-art sense of design represented in full-color magazine advertisements and on television cannot but impinge upon everyone's consciousness. (It should be noted that, with a few outstanding exceptions, those with the least knowledge of and appreciation for the visual arts are the music critics themselves.)

Finally, the visual is most blatantly served by the blockbuster productions: those spectaculars that grant the Met its role as successor to the now faded glories of Radio City Music Hall. *Die Frau ohne Schatten* was perhaps the first of these (excusing *Antony and Cleopatra*), but this year's *La Bohème* and the Olympia act of *Les Contes d'Hoffmann* are its worthy encores. It is not unusual today for ticket buyers to decide to pay not for the cast but for the production.

This shift has moved the Met in a new direction. As Samuel Lipman noted earlier, it has allowed the house to change just enough so that it does not appear dated, and it has extracted the house from the cul-de-sac imposed by the idea that singers as of yore are nonexistent, that fewer major singers devote a substantial part of their time to the Met, and that therefore opera as it once was can no longer be done.

In 1981–82 the Met played to 91.7 percent capacity—low when compared to shorter opera seasons elsewhere, but impressive over two hundred and ten performances. If "box office" has no necessary correlation to artistic value, it does point to financial health. (Yet, even so, care should be taken not to equate box office with financial health in every instance. A sold-out house for an *Aida* with a top cast and conductor may "lose" more money than an 80 percent house for a smaller-scale opera with a second-line cast, little or no chorus, and reduced orchestra.)

Artistically, the Met today is less the reflection of its general manager, Anthony Bliss, than that of his music director, James Levine. Levine's interests in repertory are the ones generally effectuated, and his concern for musicological fidelity is evidenced in at least those operas over which he has direct control. The sacrifices that he is willing to make, moreover, are ones that tend to be seconded by management. Levine may want to play every note of *La traviata* because Verdi wrote every one, but he is willing to ignore intermission breaks to make for shorter evenings (although he justifies this on musical grounds); and he is willing to put up with gross lighting distortions for the sake of nationwide television. Pragmatism, at some level, must always operate in a repertory house.

"Stability" is an important word for any organization, both internally and in terms of its posture to the outside world; and "stability" can characterize the Met today. It has meant the freedom to plan years ahead, and from an audience's point of view, the freedom to count on performance and to count on a reliable product.

Yet stability can be a curse for an artistic company, for it breeds complacency and self-satisfaction. The complaint most often heard about Met performances is their "lack of excitement." This is not strictly accurate—there is still excitement aplenty—but what is being indicated is a lack of electricity. That electricity was brought about in the past by the many changes of cast and the minimal rehearsal of so many performances, which resulted in a sense of "What will happen next?" and, quite often, a performance that surpassed its on-paper potential. If excitement on one level means the stars, on another it means risk taking, such as idiosyncratic productions of familiar works. The Met is not a risk-taking operation.

Yet the Met has never considered itself such an operation. It is a museum of great operas, dependent upon those selected to work within it and those chosen to guide it. The inordinate complexities of mounting an opera season of two hundred and ten performances can be not only wearing but debilitating, and can hobble creative thought. At the Met in 1981–82, however, I did not sense an air of despair. There was, even on the inevitable routine nights, a sense of purpose and direction, and a quiet assurance that what was being done, if hardly perfect or ideal, was at least on the right track.

Appendix

TICKET SALES 1981–1982, BY OPERA

For those who dote on statistics, the following may be of some informational use. Ticket sales in 1981–82 amounted to an aggregate of $21,093,574, of which $12,233,095 derived from subscription sales and $8,860,479 from single sales ($121,431 at a discount through the Broadway TKTS outlet and other sources). Complimentary tickets (management, press, and "comps" to fill out the house) amounted to $870,399, and there were $920,300 worth of tickets unsold. The numbers in parentheses refer to the number of performances. "Percent" refers to percentage of a full house.

	percent		percent
Il barbiere di Siviglia (10)	92.7	Parsifal (4)	83.0
La Bohème (20)	95.3	Das Rheingold (4)	97.8
Les Contes d'Hoffmann (8)	98.7	Rigoletto (15)	92.3
Così fan tutte (11)	93.5	Siegfried (6)	83.3
Die Entführung aus		Stravinsky (8)	93.3
dem Serail (7)	79.3	Tannhäuser (8)	88.9
Fidelio (6)	90.1	Tosca (9)	96.4
Die Frau ohne Schatten (5)	96.3	La traviata (15)	93.0
Hansel and Gretel (8)	63.5	Il trittico (12)	84.9
Luisa Miller (6)	98.4	Il trovatore (11)	93.9
Madama Butterfly (13)	95.7	I vespri siciliani (8)	89.2
Norma (7)	96.8	Die Zauberflöte (7)	96.9

Index

Index

A NOTE ON THE TYPE

The text of this book was set via computer-driven
cathode-ray tube in a type face called Baskerville. The
face is a facsimile reproduction of types cast from molds
made for John Baskerville (1706–75) from his designs.
Trained as a writing master, Baskerville designed distinct
and elegant type faces with sharply bracketed serifs
and a vertical emphasis. Baskerville's original
face was one of the forerunners of the type style
known as "modern face" to printers.

Composed by Centennial Graphics,
Inc., Ephrata, Pennsylvania. Printed and
bound by R. R. Donnelley & Sons Co.,
Harrisonburg, Virginia.

Designed by Sara Reynolds